CONTENTS

THE EXPLORATION OF AFRICA
FROM CAIRO TO THE CAPE

Anne Hugon

DISCOVERIES
HARRY N. ABRAMS, INC., PUBLISHERS

At the beginning of the 19th century the African interior was a terra incognita. One hundred years later the whole vast continent was under the domination of the European colonial powers. In the meantime explorers had surveyed the heart of Africa, traced the course of its rivers, charted its mountains, recorded its flora and fauna, and established links with the Africans, thus giving a new impetus to the advance of European imperialism.

CHAPTER I
A WORLD TO EXPLORE

Everything symbolic of Africa in the 18th century comes together in this allegory (left), from the frontispiece of an encyclopedia: the inevitable palm tree, the majestic lion, the "primitive" weapons, and, above all, the sensual African woman dominating the scene. The wooden statue of an explorer (right) is from the Ivory Coast.

Contrary to popular belief, the continent of Africa was
never cut off from the rest of the world. Indeed, it has
maintained contact with Asia and Europe since
prehistoric times. At the dawn of the Middle Ages Arab
caravans crossed the Sahara, carrying salt, weapons, and
cloth from north to south and bringing back gold, ivory,
and slaves in exchange. The accounts of Arab travelers
such as Ibn Battūtah (14th century), and Al-Idrisi (12th
century) are an invaluable source of information about
Africa and, specifically, the region of the Sudan.

Europeans established trading stations on the west
coast in the 15th century, exchanging manufactured
goods for exotic products and, later, slaves. Then at the
beginning of the 16th century they circumnavigated the
continent, finding that the east coast was still frequented
by Arab merchants.

Geographical Conditions Discouraged Penetration of the Interior

Knowledge of Africa was long confined to the desert zone
and the coastal regions. And even the coast was not
always easily accessible, because of the treacherous

Atlantic breakers and the
coastal swamps. But it was
above all the humid forests
of equatorial Africa that
deterred exploration, both
because of their climate and
because of the extreme
density of the vegetation.
Trees often reached
heights of nearly two
hundred feet, and axes
and machetes had to
be used to cut a path
through the tangle of
undergrowth.

Moreover, while large
centralized and organized
kingdoms did exist,
notably around the Great
Lakes, other areas were

fragmented into different linguistic, ethnic, and political groups. These divisions, which the explorers of Africa often exaggerated or generalized in order to emphasize the supposed backwardness of the continent and its peoples, proved a further obstacle to exploration.

The practical difficulties were compounded by legends calculated to deter prospective travelers. There was talk of headless monsters and of creatures half-human and half-beast—not to mention tales of cannibalistic practices sure to strike terror in the human heart.

Until the end of the 18th century the real and

The camel enabled Arab caravans, like the one pictured in this 17th-century map (above), to cross the Sahara Desert more rapidly. Travelers such as Ibn Battūtah (far left) thus acquired much knowledge of African geography in the 1300s. Left: An 1880 watercolor of a mangrove swamp.

English colonists arriving at the Cape of Good Hope in 1820 (left). This 15th-century map of the world (below) shows a confusion of the Nile and the Niger, which are shown joining at the latitude of the African kingdoms, represented by tents.

imagined perils of Africa discouraged Europeans from exploring the interior. What, in any case, would have been the point? The main reason for travel to Africa during the previous three centuries was the slave traffic, and contact with the coastal areas was quite sufficient for this purpose. In 1790 there were no more than 25,000 Europeans on the entire continent, and these were all concentrated on the coast (21,000 of them at the Cape of Good Hope).

Yet it was at this stage that European interest in Africa began to develop in a new direction. A number of factors were to alter radically the relationship of the two continents by the end of the century.

It was Great Britain that first turned toward Africa with new eyes. When it came to fighting the slave trade and exploring the continent, the British were the real pioneers.

Scientific Inquiry and Geographical Curiosity

At the end of the Age of Enlightenment (or the Age of Reason, as the 18th century was also known), the public and explorers alike were fascinated by the "great blanks on the map of Africa," as French explorer

Louis-Gustave Binger described them. Until then cartographers had had no option but to imagine the interior of the continent. The courses of African rivers were pure fantasy: On these maps the Nile joined the Niger, and the Congo was an unassuming little coastal river.

These fictions soon ceased to satisfy the growing scientific expectations of an educated public. In 1788 a booklet was issued in London by the newly formed Association for Promoting the Discovery of the Interior Parts of Africa (or the African Association). It stated that at least one third of the inhabited surface of the earth was unknown, notably Africa, virtually in its entirety. For the first time this ignorance was seen as a shameful gap in human knowledge that must immediately be filled.

But geographical curiosity was not the only motive. The European elite—stirred by the discoveries of Sir Isaac Newton, the writings of René Descartes and Francis Bacon, and Denis Diderot's publication in 1751 of the first encyclopedia—was becoming increasingly fascinated by science and in particular by ethnography, which was still in its infancy at the time.

Interest in the facts of the natural world was not, however, an end in itself. Toward the end of the 18th century, it was believed to be the mission of human reason to achieve perfect mastery of the world by discovering the laws of the universe. Thus the African Association, resolutely

Naturalist Sir Joseph Banks (1743–1820) accompanied fellow Briton Captain James Cook (1728–79) on his explorations of the Pacific in 1768. Banks founded the African Association twenty years later. Son of a prominent trader, he had a network of scientific advisers and a substantial following, including the Prince of Wales. Below: Slaves in eastern Africa, drawn by Scottish missionary and explorer David Livingstone.

up-to-date in its optimism, proclaimed its conviction in the usefulness and purpose of enlarging human knowledge through the exploration of Africa.

The Age of the Abolitionists

At the same time a humanist philanthropic movement was emerging in Europe. Exploration of the Pacific Ocean had focused Europeans' attention on previously unknown civilizations, and the writings of certain travelers fostered a belief in so-called primitive cultures as models of social harmony. The myth of the "noble savage" came into fashion, and with it there developed a newfound sympathy for remote civilizations.

On a practical level, industrialists opposed slavery, considering it an obstacle to the emergence of a modern industrial capitalism based on free labor; it was, simply, unprofitable. Already in a superior economic situation, England hoped to weaken its European rivals by its opposition to the slave trade. At the same time public outcries against slavery on moral grounds— especially in Great Britain and the United States—began to be heard. Those in positions

This illustration of an abolitionist petition is taken from *The Black Man's Lament*, by Amelia Opie, published in 1826. The slave trade was fought by many methods, including organized petitions and engravings aimed at changing public opinion. This 19th-century abolitionist engraving (left) shows a black man in chains. Full of good intentions and with strong beliefs in a common humanity, many abolitionists were nonetheless highly paternalistic: Whites and blacks were undoubtedly brothers and sisters, it was said, but Europeans took the role of older siblings—thus, a so-called benevolent racism.

of influence, motivated by both economic and ideological concerns, rebelled at the idea that their compatriots were actively involved in the selling of fellow human beings. In denouncing this legal traffic in slaves and calling for its abolition, Americans, the English, and other Europeans began to take a closer interest in the peoples of Africa. Opponents of the traffic saw the realization of their hopes at the Congress of Vienna in 1814–5, where Great Britain and France, among others, acknowledged in principle that the slave trade should be abolished.

This decision was largely based on philosophical grounds, even though learned Europeans remained for the most part deeply ignorant of African societies. Seeking to promote "civilization" and happiness on the continent, many ignored the individual characters of African cultures. Even the Scottish missionary David Livingstone, who was little given to disparaging the Africans, betrayed a well-meaning condescension when he wrote that his object was to help the people of Africa to "take a place among the nations of the Earth."

Abolitionists gathered at large meetings like that shown in this painting by Benjamin Robert Haydon, *Anti-Slavery Society Convention,* 1840. Though it was illegal in British territories from 1830 onward, slavery nonetheless continued to be practiced. Abolitionists recruited their supporters, men and women, from the upper classes and industrial and business circles. The latter regarded the abolition of slavery as a factor in economic progress.

   This patronizing attitude was based on the undoubted, and recent, technological advances of the Western world, in which Europeans quickly saw an indication of their own moral superiority.

Missionaries Discovered Africa: A New Land in Which to Spread the Gospel

Well before the 18th century, European missionaries had tried to introduce Christianity to parts of Africa. Toward the end of the 15th and the beginning of the 16th centuries their efforts were concentrated specifically in the Congo and Angola. The particularly dynamic Portuguese made remarkable efforts but met with scant success. And for a time the disappointed church fathers lost interest in the fate of the Africans.

   At the end of the 18th century, leaders of the Christian

Missionaries and laypeople alike were quick to realize that illustrations stimulated the reader's imagination, enlivening what otherwise might be an unexciting text. Most travel writings published in Europe were amply illustrated, often by the artistically gifted author-explorers. This engraving (above) is from *Travels, Researches, and Missionary Labours During an Eighteen Years' Residence in Eastern Africa* by Johann L. Krapf.

In their writings the missionaries laid much emphasis on their good works. The school, the dispensary, and, of course, the church were the main arenas of evangelical activity. Livingstone explained what was required for a conversion: No one was baptized unless he or she could read and understand the nature of the Christian religion. But as Livingstone himself observed, Christianity was not always embraced for purely spiritual motives. There were some, he lamented, who professed the faith for material gain. Missions often happened to have a store of manufactured goods (tools and cloth, for example) which were given to converts in payment for their work. Below: Livingstone preaching in South Africa, 1877.

world rather belatedly decided that the slave trade was inconsistent with its aspirations and teachings, whereupon a number of missionaries once again set out for the African unknown to spread the Gospel.

British clergy saw Africa as a continent awaiting redemption. In the 19th century the influence of preachers increased, and there was no shortage of volunteers, in spite of the fact that the Europeans were vulnerable to tropical diseases and, once exposed, died in large numbers. Yet, while they had health problems, there was no need to worry about money. In the course of the century the missionary societies accumulated considerable funds, thanks to donations by the faithful, who saw that support for the works of the church could win them social

The numerous Christian missions competed, sometimes acrimoniously, for African territories. There was rivalry not only between the Roman Catholic church and the Reformed churches but also between the various Protestant sects. Often the conflicts were exacerbated by competition among the various European nations: Catholic missions were predominantly French, and Protestant ones generally American, English, or German. The missionaries did not live entirely in native African style; they incorporated European customs and other elements into their households. These Christian outposts thus brought new—and not purely religious— cultural influences and tastes to Africa. This watercolor, dated 1880, is of the Mbweni mission in Zanzibar.

Overleaf: A 1908 watercolor showing the interior of the missionary Bishop Weston's house.

Perpetual snow at the equator on Mount Kenya and Mount Kilimanjaro (left), in an engraving from Johann L. Krapf's *Travels* (1869). These mountains captured the imagination of Europeans, who dreamed of the gold and diamonds awaiting them in Africa. This engraving of men washing gold-bearing sand (below) is dated 1820.

esteem. The missionary society of the Church of England, for example, saw its annual income increase five-fold between 1830 and 1875.

Two German missionaries, Johann Ludwig Krapf and Johannes Rebmann, were among the pioneers in central Africa. Arriving in Mombasa (Kenya) in 1840, they translated the Bible into Swahili to help gain converts. They were the first Europeans to mention the snowcapped peaks of Mount Kenya and Mount Kilimanjaro. Geographers at home, however, remained unconvinced by their discoveries.

Unlike Krapf and Rebmann, the majority of missionaries tended to be more sedentary than exploratory. Nonetheless, in establishing Christian outposts in remote areas, some of them sent home word of their discoveries. The most famous of these was, of course, David Livingstone, though they all did much to make Europeans better acquainted with Africa through their published writings and talks.

The Aspirations of Merchants

Banning the slave trade did not stop it continuing illegally. The volume was nevertheless substantially reduced over the course of the century. Some European slave traffickers were obliged to consider alternative occupations, while others gradually came to realize the potential benefits of trade with an Africa that was more fully integrated into the international commercial network. Indeed, the "Dark Continent" seemed capable of supplying exotic products in large quantities: palm oil, an ingredient in soap, and a type of gum that was used in pharmaceuticals, to mention just two. In addition, Africa had considerable mineral resources to whet the appetite of the Europeans. Livingstone described bars of copper up to a hundred pounds in weight circulating in Katanga (Congo). Industrial Europe began to nurse dreams of controlling its sources of raw materials.

Europeans also came to realize that Africa could become an important market for manufactured goods, particularly with the opening up of the continent's

Africa-shaped nugget from the Congo.

interior. Factories needed outlets for their products, so every prospective new market was to be welcomed.

But the potential markets and sources of raw materials had to be reached before they could be developed. Whole regions were still undiscovered and unmapped, and contact had to be established with the African peoples. A strong dose of humanism was thus allied to a shrewd and pragmatic commercial sense. Together they led to the exploration of the African interior.

Beginning at the End of the 19th Century Exploration and Colonization Went Hand in Hand

In the 1880s the European powers began to see the advantages of establishing a permanent presence in Africa. Political control of the continent would give them increased prestige, great economic advantages, and

At the end of the 18th century London was the financial center of the world. Here intellectual and commercial interest in Africa was concentrated. Thomas Allom's picture (above) shows the Port of London in the 19th century. But it was England's second port, Liverpool, that built its fortunes on traffic with the "Dark Continent." Initially involved in the slave trade, it turned to less heinous commerce in the 19th century. A number of explorers sailed from Liverpool on steamships of the merchant navy. The transportation of ivory is the subject of this 19th-century French illustration (left).

guarantees of future prosperity. While explorers had until this time been financed by private institutions, from 1880 on numerous expeditions were wholly or partially backed by governments. The scramble for colonies was under way.

The explorations, led by officers, were usually military in character and systematically organized. These officer-explorers acted as ambassadors whose task was to defend their national flag against foreign competition. When they set out to explore unknown territories, their primary and official goal was to sign treaties with the African kings and chiefs. Geographical curiosity was of secondary concern, notably in the case of the French, who enjoined their soldiers and noncommissioned officers to win the sympathy of the rulers with the object of establishing a protectorate in their territories. The exploration of the African continent was therefore inextricably linked to its colonization, whatever might have been the wishes of the individual explorers themselves.

These sometimes indistinguishable motives

Pierre Savorgnan de Brazza (above) and Jean-Baptiste Marchand (below) had brilliant careers in Africa.

can be summed up by a list of five easily remembered words: curiosity, civilization, christianization, commerce, and colonization.

Thus, various in its aims and motivation, the new interest in Africa at the end of the 19th century is aptly symbolized by the figure of the explorer, pioneer of unknown regions.

A Typically European Figure

The very word *explorer* suggests almost a caricature—a figure, pith helmet firmly on his head, still bravely leading his expedition in spite of exhaustion. Relentlessly hunting big game or elephants, contending with mosquitoes and other nefarious insects, he never abandons his ultimate goal. By turns debonair and commanding, resolute and cautious, enthusiastic and disillusioned, he is the all-around hero, scornful above all else of deceit and irresolution.

In reality explorers were much more complex figures, greatly circumscribed by the historical context. European or North American, men and women, they had, first of all, a precise social function: to inform contemporaries about the state of the world while reinforcing the image of white superiority over other races. They had access to knowledge, thanks to their presumed qualities of courage and self-sacrifice.

No African expedition was complete without its shooting trophies. Game hunting was particularly popular with the British, the elephant being the most prestigious quarry. It was also a way of impressing the natives. Left: Portuguese explorer Alexandre Serpa Pinto hunting lions, 1877.

Explorers were representatives of the "civilized" world in central Africa.

And yet—and this is not the only paradox in their situation—these travelers were often rebels against their own communities. Constricted by the conventions of 19th-century society, particularly those of Victorian England, they longed for a freer way of life. In leaving home to explore a world as different from their own as Africa, they escaped the rules and constraints that weighed on them so heavily.

Sir Richard Burton, for instance, never felt at home among the Victorians and was often accused of being

This watercolor by explorer Samuel Baker is of the Latooka funeral dance. Foreigners were often greeted with ceremonies that they found fascinating but incomprehensible.

"un-British." Passionately interested in non-European cultures, he was considered both a renegade and a brilliant explorer in the service of Great Britain. Mary Kingsley also felt considerable reservations about the over-civilized society in which she had grown up. She fled England and declared tropical Africa to be her homeland—while remaining, of course, steeped in Victorian values.

S ir Richard Burton (below left) deliberately cultivated an Eastern character and image. His penchant for opium, taste for dissolute company, and reputation for homosexuality compromised his military career and outraged his contemporaries. The decoration of his house in Trieste, Italy, shows his taste for the Eastern bazaar.

The Explorers Were Not Immune to Popular Notions of Africa

The majority of the explorers were, in different ways, incurable romantics. Some were drawn by the prospect of a total change of

scene. Concerned exclusively with novelty and strangeness, they perceived Africa as the exact antithesis of the Western world. Others, driven by the desire to test themselves to the limit of their endurance, regarded it as their path to salvation.

The fascination the continent exerted was linked to the mysterious character it had assumed. In the European imagination it was the land of dark forces, inaccessible places, and extraordinary peoples. Its fascination was charged with an element of fear that increased the prestige of the explorers even further.

O pposite: Sir Henry Morton Stanley, the archetypal explorer, stands proud and determined, gun in hand, ready to face the equatorial forest.

They themselves fostered this image by readily speaking of the "dark" or the "mysterious" continent. As a whole the explorers, like their contemporaries, entertained a vision of Africa that was colored more by fantasy than by reality.

The Work of the Explorers Was a Work of Creation

Once they had returned successfully, travelers enjoyed great status in the Western world. It seemed as if rivers, towns, and mountains could be said to exist only once they had been "discovered" and named by European explorers. Conveniently forgetting that the Africans were already well acquainted with their native lands, the explorers had no hesitation in claiming to be the "first" to climb this mountain or the "first" to follow that river to

O verleaf: British explorer John Hanning Speke's map of the Ujiji region of Tanzania (left above). Livingstone's maps of Victoria Falls (left below) and Lake Shirwa (right).

its source, as if they had just set foot on an uninhabited planet. In the same spirit they "christened" lakes and waterfalls, deliberately ignoring their existing names, which were, of course, full of meaning.

The waterfalls of the Zambezi, for example, known to the native population for self-evident reasons as the "smoke that thunders" (*Mosioatunya*), became known as Victoria Falls after Livingstone reached them in 1855. In this way the Europeans symbolically appropriated the places they discovered.

The choice of the new names was highly significant.

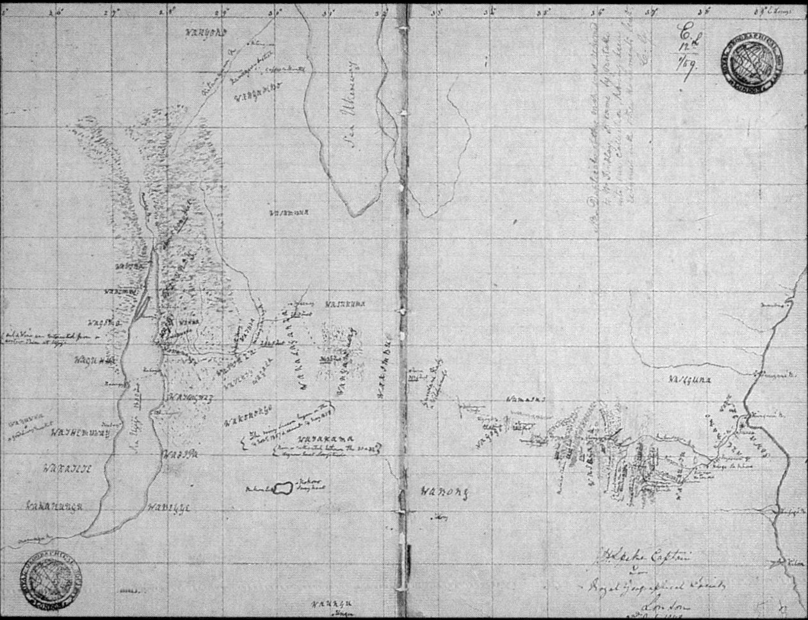
Sea Ukerewe
WAKERONGO
WANONG
WAHEHE
Royal Geographical Society London

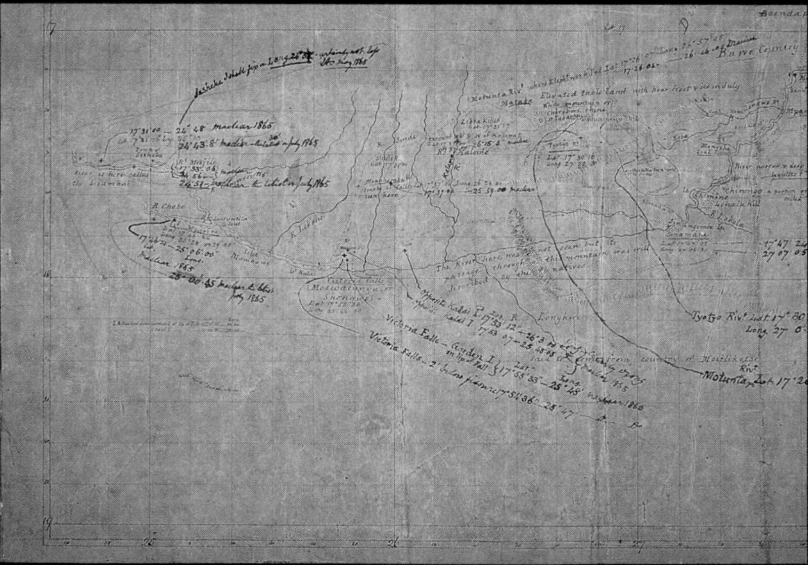
Bawe Country
Elevated table land with hoar frost visible in July
R. Chobe
R. Kalomo
The River here was not seen but its passage through this mountain was well described by the natives
Victoria Falls
Tyotyo Rivr
Motunta

37

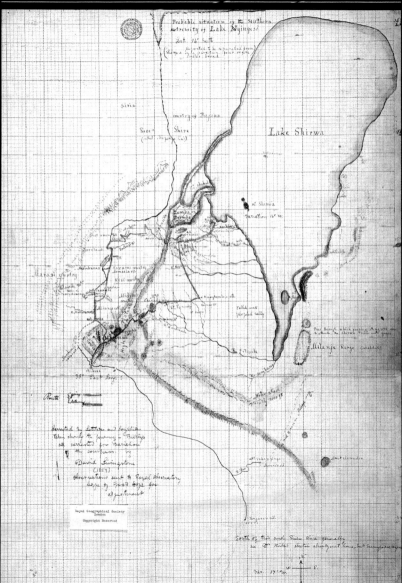

The entire British royal family came to be associated with the geography of central Africa: In addition to Victoria Falls, there were Lake Victoria, Lake Albert, Lake Edward, and Lake George. Some travelers humbly paid tribute to those who had helped them realize their projects. Murchison and Ripon Falls thus made their appearance on the map, named after two presidents of the Royal Geographical Society in London. Other explorers, with less modesty, went as far as to name the sites they discovered after themselves: Henry Morton Stanley, for example (Mount Stanley and Stanley Falls). The explorers began to see themselves almost as divine creators of all they discovered.

Sir Roderick Impey Murchison (above), geologist, was president of the Royal Geographical Society several times between 1843 and his death in 1871. Wealthy, methodical, and authoritarian, like many who worked for the advancement of science, he encouraged expeditions to find the source of the Nile. Samuel Baker christened Murchison Falls in tribute to him. This illustration of the falls (right) is after one of Baker's drawings.

Left: Queen Victoria with seven of her nine children, in a painting by John Calcott Horsley. To impress African rulers, the British explorers John Hanning Speke and James Augustus Grant, among others, had no scruples in claiming to be her sons.

In the 5th century BC Greek historian Herodotus wrote, "Egypt is a gift from the Nile." This river, which played so essential a role in Egyptian civilization that it was regarded as divine, remained a geographical mystery for centuries. Its source was said to lie at the very edge of the world—and perhaps even beyond. It was only in the 19th century, after much floundering, that explorers began to be able to solve the mystery.

CHAPTER II
THE MYSTERY OF THE SOURCE OF THE NILE

Englishman John Hanning Speke (left, in a portrait by James Watney Wilson) was the true discoverer of the source of the Nile. But he had great difficulty convincing the rest of the world. He was denied the fame enjoyed by less talented explorers.

Pursuing the questions raised by the Greeks, Roman Emperor Nero (AD 37–68) sent an expedition to track the Nile to its source. It may have reached the Sudd, a swampy region in southern Sudan. This illustration of the cataracts of the Nile (left) comes from Frédéric Cailliaud's account of his travels.

Since antiquity curious minds had wondered about the source of the longest river in the world, the river that had witnessed the rise of a fascinating civilization.

Reports from Antiquity

Tough geographical conditions made it difficult to establish the answer to the question. The six cataracts upstream of Aswan, in southern Egypt, prevented navigation, and the Nile seemed to lose itself inextricably in the marshes of the Sudanese lowlands, at a latitude of some 8° N, making it impossible to track the river to its source.

The Greek historian Herodotus compounded traditional erroneous hypotheses by confusing the Niger and the Nile. According to him, they were

one and the same river, which had its source in western Africa and flowed across Chad toward Egypt. This theory had its adherents until quite a late date.

Meanwhile another Greek, Ptolemy, put forward a more accurate version of the facts in the 2nd century AD. An astronomer and geographer, Ptolemy consulted the works of a predecessor, Marinus of Tyre, in the Alexandria library. At the end of the 1st century AD Marinus had drawn on the writings of Diogenes, who had earlier explored the east coast of Africa. Using this evidence Ptolemy drew a map featuring high, snow-covered mountains: the Mountains of the

A bove: This 15th-century illustration shows Ptolemy consulting one of the 700,000 tomes in the Alexandria library, the largest repository of scientific information in antiquity. Throughout the Middle Ages people drew, more or less faithfully, upon his work.

In the 15th century Ptolemy's famous *Geography* was translated into Latin, inspiring maps that reproduced the Africa of the Ancients (left): an imagined continent, of which only the northern regions were known. Ignorance of the south was total, and the western coastline was uncertain. The Nile, however, was fairly accurately sited. Still, people were reluctant to believe in Ptolemy rather than Herodotus.

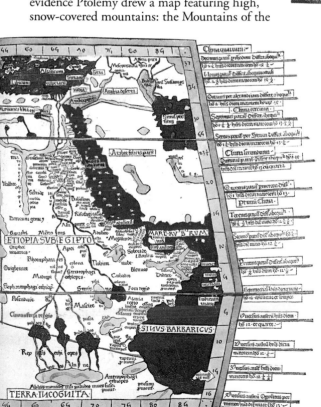

Moon (Ruwenzori). At their base lakes spread northward, giving birth to a river. Downstream a tributary flowing from another lake joined the Nile at the latitude of Meroë, in central Sudan.

Contrary to all expectations, the discoveries that took place in the 19th century corroborated "this map of highly suspect origin" (in the words of French historian Hubert Deschamps). The ancients had in fact correctly surmised the basic configuration of the upper reaches of the Nile: the high mountains, the role of the lakes, the existence of a tributary on the right bank. This tributary greatly complicated the explorations, for it meant that there were in fact two rivers to be discovered: the White Nile, with its source in the heart of Africa, and the Blue Nile, originating in Ethiopia.

Diogenes had also realized that it would be fruitless to sail up the Nile, and he wrote that investigations had to start from the shores of the Indian Ocean. This indeed was the course followed by the 19th-century explorers.

The Blue Nile, shorter, less regular, and less mysterious than the White Nile, was nonetheless important. Flowing from the high plateaus of Ethiopia, it carried down tons of fertilizing lime and dispersed them on the Egyptian banks to the great benefit of agriculture. This view of the Hawash River is taken from *Scenes in Ethiopia* (1852), by John Martin Bernatz.

The Source of the Blue Nile Was the First to Be Traced

The first explorers were fired as much by the desire for glory as by scientific curiosity. Among them was James Bruce (1730–94), a stalwart and well-born Scotsman with a passionate interest in unknown lands.

In the 1760s, after serving as British consul in North Africa, he set off for Ethiopia (then known as Abyssinia), where he hoped to discover the source of the Nile. He studied the Ethiopian language and learned to handle the scientific instruments useful in exploration. Having landed on the western shore of the Red Sea, he made his way to Gonder, capital of a powerful Ethiopian kingdom then suffering political disturbances. He observed the local life and customs, staying in the court of the Negus, and then traveled to the volcanic Lake Tana, which gives rise to the spectacular water-falls of Tisisat. Convinced that this was the beginning of the Nile, Bruce went up the course of the Little Abbai, a river feeding the lake. Reaching its source, he claimed to have settled the mystery of the source of the Nile.

In fact he had traced only the source of the Blue Nile, the great river's main tributary. This was a relatively minor achievement, as other Westerners had been there before him. Two Portuguese

James Bruce (below) maintained a correspondence with a host of scholars. This came in handy when he lost his instruments at sea and the French naturalist Georges de Buffon was able to persuade Louis XV to send replacements. The flora and fauna illustrated above were seen by Bruce in Ethiopia.

Jesuits, Francisco Alvarez and Pedro Paez, were the first Europeans to have explored the Blue Nile, as long ago as the 16th and 17th centuries. Bruce tried to discredit his predecessors. A convinced Protestant, he felt nothing but contempt for the Catholic fathers, puppets of Rome. His religious prejudice was compounded by an element of national chauvinism. It was vexing to have been preceded by the Portuguese when he had dedicated his own "discovery" to his sovereign, King George III.

Bruce is in fact remarkable more for his writings and ethnographic observations than for his geographical discoveries. In *Travels to Discover the Source of the Nile 1768–73,* published in 1790, he gives a detailed description of the life and customs of the Ethiopians and comes to the conclusion that, despite the apparent exoticism of the manners he depicts, human nature is the same everywhere. His work is embellished with numerous plates and illustrations of Ethiopian fauna and flora and remains a useful source of information on the history of the country, although Bruce's contemporaries suspected him of exaggeration and even of inventing part of his report.

Cailliaud and the Egyptian Expedition

The Europeans were not alone in their curiosity about the course of the Nile south of the Sudanese basin. At the beginning of the 19th century the Egyptians tried to resolve the mystery by going up the river themselves. Between 1820 and 1822 Muhammad Ali Pasha, viceroy of Egypt, sent an expedition to the Nile. It was joined by the French explorer Frédéric Cailliaud, who reached the junction of the two rivers and established that the Blue Nile was a tributary of the great Nile. The expedition went no higher than Gondokoro, in southern Sudan. The source of the White Nile would be found many hundreds of miles further south.

The British to the Fore

In the 1850s Great Britain sought tighter control over the east coast of Africa. Its influence in Zanzibar grew after 1856, when the island declared independence from the sultanate of Oman as a result of pressure from the British. Their interest increased as exploration of the interior took them into central Africa, extending their power from Cairo to the Cape.

In 1857 two British officers sent by the Royal Geographical Society (RGS) and the Foreign Office embarked on the quest for the sources of the Nile. Theirs was an official mission, not a private initiative. The highly respected RGS was the direct successor of the African

The opening of the Suez Canal (above) in 1869 linked the Mediterranean directly to the Red Sea and helped Europe to increase its stranglehold on East Africa. The British government was from 1875 the main shareholder: The canal shortened the route from England to India by some five thousand miles—the principal reason for British interest.

Frédéric Cailliaud, archaeologist and geologist, marveled at all he saw: giraffes, ostriches, the peoples of the Nile (shown, left, in traditional dress), the vestiges of the vanished civilization of Meroë, and the Absyr cataract on the Nile (far left).

Association, which had sent Scotsman Mungo Park to find the course of the Niger River in West Africa in 1795.

John Hanning Speke (1827–64) and Richard Burton (1821–90), who were chosen to lead the 1857 expedition, were both officers in the Indian Army. Each had already distinguished himself in similar ventures. The RGS did not entrust its missions to amateurs.

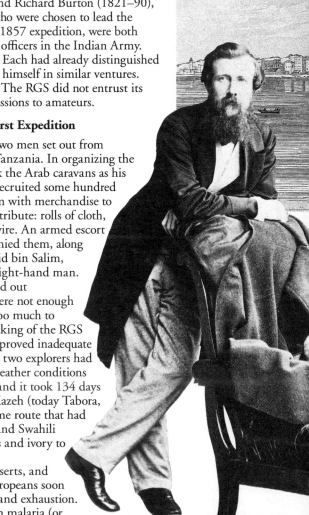

Burton and Speke's First Expedition

On 16 June 1857 the two men set out from Bagamoyo, in eastern Tanzania. In organizing the expedition, Burton took the Arab caravans as his models. The explorers recruited some hundred porters and loaded them with merchandise to be used in paying local tribute: rolls of cloth, glass beads, and brass wire. An armed escort of thirty men accompanied them, along with an Arab guide, Said bin Salim, who became Burton's right-hand man.

The expedition started out inauspiciously. There were not enough porters, and they had too much to carry. The financial backing of the RGS and the Foreign Office proved inadequate to pay the 175 men the two explorers had requested. Disastrous weather conditions delayed the departure, and it took 134 days for the party to reach Kazeh (today Tabora, Tanzania) along the same route that had been trodden by Arab and Swahili merchants taking slaves and ivory to the coast.

Crossing marshes, deserts, and mountains, the two Europeans soon succumbed to sickness and exhaustion. They were afflicted with malaria (or

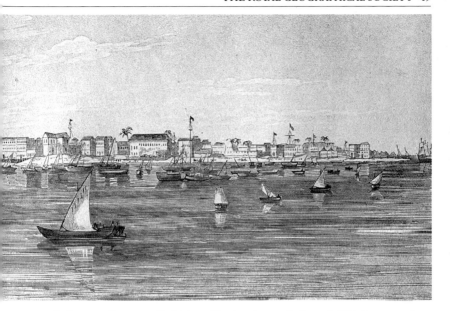

marsh fever, as Burton called it) and had to be carried on litters. At Kazeh they were forced to stop and recuperate. The expedition then continued on its way west, ignoring the advice an Arab gave Burton to go north in the direction of a lake called Nyanza.

On 13 February 1858, after eight months en route, the two men finally sighted an immense expanse of water: Lake Tanganyika (Tanzania). They are thought to be the first Europeans to set eyes on it. Illness forced them to stop at Ujiji, a trading town on the shore of the lake. Speke was temporarily blind as the result of an eye infection, and Burton, who could not eat properly because of an abscess on his tongue, was virtually paralyzed.

They nonetheless explored the northern shore of Lake Tanganyika in search of its outlet, and established that the river they had been told about, the Ruzizi, flowed into the lake rather than out of it. Speke also estimated that the altitude of the lake (about 2500 feet) was too low for it to feed the Nile. Disappointment followed their initial feelings of exaltation.

This illustration of Zanzibar (above) is from Richard Burton's *The Lake Regions of Central Africa* (1860).

John Hanning Speke, big-game hunter extraordinaire (left), was also a trained botanist and geologist. His travels in the Himalayas and Tibet gave him a taste for adventure and developed his exceptional instincts as an explorer.

The drawing opposite above shows No. 1 Savile Row, London, home of the RGS from 1871 to 1913.

R ichard Burton was irresistibly drawn to the Orient and exotic adventures. His first exploit was to enter Mecca disguised as an Afghan pilgrim (opposite). He then penetrated the forbidden city of Harar (above left) in the horn of Africa. A brilliant linguist, he spoke over thirty languages, including Arabic and Hindustani, and translated the *Arabian Nights* and erotic Indian texts. An overweening ambition went with a difficult character. Burton was demanding, proud, authoritarian, and irascible, with an utter disregard for conventional values, which led him to end his days as a minor diplomat. This photograph (above) was taken at the end of his life, when he was living in Trieste (left).

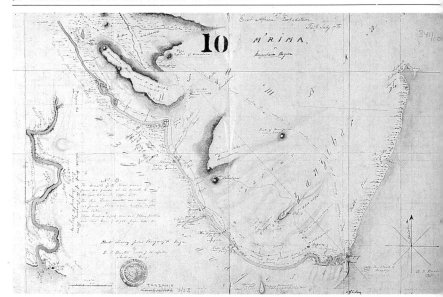

Speke's Solitary Voyage

In May Speke and Burton continued their journey and stopped again at Kazeh. Relations between the two men had markedly deteriorated. The great physical suffering they had undergone served to sour their tempers and exacerbate their incompatibility. Speke therefore decided to head north on his own in quest of another lake. Burton was left to regain his health and to gather information about the region.

Reaching Mwanza (north Tanzania) on 3 August 1858, Speke discovered what amounted to an inland sea; the largest lake in Africa (26,200 square miles) stretched before his eyes. (In fact, there is only one larger freshwater lake in the world—Lake Superior.) Deliberately ignoring its African name, he christened it Lake Victoria in honor of his queen. Wasting no time in exploring the region, he returned to Kazeh and announced that he had found the source of the Nile. It was at this stage no more than an intuition, but one that proved to be true. Burton had no words harsh

The map above charts Speke and Burton's route from Zanzibar to Fuga.

"Nothing, in sooth, could be more picturesque than this first view of the Tanganyika Lake, as it lay in the lap of the mountains, basking in the gorgeous tropical sunshine.... Forgetting toils, dangers, and the doubtfulness of return, I felt willing to endure double what I had endured."

Richard Burton,
The Lake Regions of Central Africa, 1860

enough to express his scorn for these claims. He was utterly convinced that the source of the river lay in the direction of Kilimanjaro.

In February 1859 the two explorers, now sworn enemies, parted company at Zanzibar. Speke returned to England and informed the Royal Geographical Society of his discovery.

Useful instruments, illustrated in Speke's journal (above), and (left) his map of Lake Nyasa and Lake Tanganyika. The donkey, often ridden by explorers (below), was ungratefully described by Burton: "Stubborn, vicious, and guilty of the four mortal sins of the equine race, he shies and stumbles, he rears and runs away."

The resulting excitement matched the occasion. A mystery dating back to antiquity itself had just been solved! Burton, bitter and excluded from Speke's success, published his own account of the voyage: *The Lake Regions of Central Africa* (1860), a mine of ethnographic and topographic information. And he embarked on a ferocious feud with his erstwhile companion.

Speke Persuaded the Royal Geographical Society to Entrust Him with a New Mission

The dispute between the two men fascinated geographers. Famous explorers took sides in the quarrel, among them David Livingstone, who wrongly supported Burton's views. Speke decided to undertake another expedition as the only way of convincing his opponents. Sir Roderick Murchison, one of the founders and then president of the RGS, gave him £2000 toward the financing of his project.

Burned by his experience with Burton, Speke chose as his fellow traveler a more amenable character, James Augustus Grant (1827–92), who had also been an officer in the Indian Army. The caravan this time numbered seventy-six porters—on departure at any rate; on arrival there were no more than eighteen. The majority deserted because of the excessively harsh conditions imposed on them.

Setting out from Zanzibar in October 1860, Speke traveled over already-familiar ground and reached Kazeh without difficulty along the same route he had taken in 1857. From there the caravan headed for the shores of Victoria Nyanza (Lake Victoria), in Tanzania, northwest of which lay the kingdom of Buganda, ruled by King Mutesa.

Speke and Grant then decided to go in different directions. Grant headed north toward the kingdom of Bunyoro, while Speke turned slightly eastward, following the contours of the lake.

On 28 July 1862 Speke reached the far north of Victoria Nyanza and there found great rapids, as he had been led to expect. This was the spot where the legendary

Mutesa, ruler of Buganda, was reviled by Speke and admired by Stanley.

Speke worked better with Grant than with the impossible Burton. Here we see the departure of their caravan. They discovered the Kagera, the main tributary of Lake Victoria. Opposite above: A watercolor by Speke.

river emerged from the lake. And Speke had proved his 1857 intuition: The Nile, in fact, did flow out of Lake Victoria. In tribute to the Royal Geographical Society, which had enabled him to make his great discovery, Speke named Ripon Falls after Earl de Grey and Ripon, president of the society in late 1859.

The explorer was greatly tempted to investigate the

"The expedition had now performed its functions. I saw that old father Nile without any doubt rises in the Victoria Nyanza, and, as I had foretold, that lake is the great source of the holy river which cradled the first expounder of our religious belief," wrote Speke in his journal on reaching Ripon Falls (left).

region more thoroughly. But time was short. He and Grant were due to meet a supply party at Gondokoro, a trading station on the banks of the upper Nile dealing in slaves and ivory. Speke therefore returned to Bunyoro, where he met Grant.

Together, Speke and Grant traveled across Egypt with those of their men who had not yet deserted. From Cairo they sent a cable to London claiming to have found the source of the Nile. This was, of course, an overstatement. Ripon Falls turned out not to be the ultimate source of the river; the watercourse that fed the lake had yet to be explored.

The challenge ahead was to convince the skeptics. A meeting between Speke and Burton was arranged at the Royal Geographical Society in September 1864. Tragically, the day before it was due to take place Speke died in a shooting accident, which was regarded by some as suicide. The incident troubled many people and confirmed Livingstone in his belief that Speke had been wrong.

Speke and Grant Had Found Only One Missing Piece in the Puzzle of Central Africa

Another Englishman, Samuel Baker (1821–93), like Speke and Grant a former officer in the Indian Army, also aspired to win fame in these regions. Speke and Grant had on their return journey happened upon Baker and his wife, Florence, at Gondokoro. In fact, this apparently

accidental meeting owed nothing to chance.

In 1863, following a request by the Royal Geographical Society, Samuel Baker had been sent by the British consul in Khartoum (Sudan), John Petherick, to look for Speke and Grant, who had erroneously been reported missing. Aboard little steam launches, the Bakers sailed up the Nile to Gondokoro.

Although they'd duly found Speke and Grant, the Bakers decided their mission wasn't accomplished. They'd heard that northwest of Victoria Nyanza there was a second lake, known as Luta Nzigé. Fired by enthusiasm, the Bakers set off to find it, heedless of the difficulties of the journey. It took them almost a year to cover a mere four hundred miles.

They had to travel with a slave caravan to make any progress at all. They lacked quinine and were thus vulnerable to malaria. Their food supplies ran low, and their pack animals died, one after another.

This 1880 engraving shows Speke, Grant, and the Bakers at Gondokoro. Speke described their meeting: "Walking down the bank of the river—where a line of vessels was moored… we saw hurrying toward us the form of an Englishman, who, for a moment, we believed was Simon Pure; but the next moment my old friend Baker, famed for his sports in Ceylon, seized me by the hand."

The Bakers' Discovery of Another Great Inland Lake Further Complicated the Geographical Picture

At last they reached Mrooli, capital of Bunyoro, where the chief, Kamrasi, received

More rapturous still was the reception given for Speke and Grant at the Royal Geographical Society (left) on their return to England. The president awarded them a medal at a gathering of enthusiastic admirers. The society held special evenings devoted to Africa. These were very popular, particularly when attended by well-known explorers.

Samuel Baker was born in 1821 to a prosperous family. Educated by tutors, not at fashionable schools, he soon emerged as an individualist with conservative leanings. His experience of distant countries did little to broaden his mind. Drawn by feats of arms, big-game hunting, and physical challenge, he traveled in Ceylon (Sri Lanka) and the Balkans before visiting Africa. The spread of British dominance in so many countries amounted in his eyes to proof of British superiority. It did not take the racist theories of the 19th century to convince him that Anglo-Saxons were the elite of humanity. Xenophobia colored his writings, which consist largely of singing his own praises. This criticism cannot, however, be leveled at his artistic works. This watercolor is of himself and his wife at Shoa. On the following pages is another watercolor, also by Baker, of warriors and shepherds in the Shire River region.

them with the honor due to Speke's "brothers" and initially refused to let them leave.

King Kamrasi in fact suspected the Bakers of nursing secret political plans. A dynastic quarrel was raging in the kingdom, and the foreigners' weapons could well have been intended to overthrow him in favor of a rival. Furthermore, the sovereign was skeptical about the expedition's declared purpose, which in his eyes was wholly absurd. His reaction is a revealing clue to the yawning cultural gulf between the two sides. A traditional story recorded at the beginning of the 20th century says: "He knew that the stranger lied, because one does not leave one's country and one's people, defying exhaustion and danger, in order merely to admire a stretch of water." The misunderstanding was aggravated by the fact that Samuel Baker, convinced of the racial superiority of white people, was not prepared to submit to the authority of an African. The situation became very strained.

Eventually the Bakers managed to leave Bunyoro and headed west with their little caravan. On 14 March 1864 they reached the shores of another lake feeding the waters of the White Nile: the famous Luta Nzigé, which they renamed Lake Albert after Queen Victoria's husband. Baker believed that what he saw in front of him was the second source of the Nile, but he never confirmed this, as he failed to specify how

Florence Baker (left) had no ordinary life. Taken prisoner by the Turks in her native Hungary, she found herself in a Turkish slave market, where Baker spotted and bought her. From that moment on, they never separated. He constantly praised her courage and sangfroid in the face of danger.

This watercolor (left) by Baker is of the Obbo war dance. He wrote in *The Albert Nyanza* (1866): "I will exhibit a picture of the savage man precisely as he is; as I saw him; and as I judged him, free from prejudice.... The journey is long, the countries savage...all is wild and brutal, hard and unfeeling, devoid of that holy instinct instilled by nature into the heart of man." In this engraving (below) King Kamrasi's envoys acknowledge Baker, declaring him to be Speke's "brother."

the lake fed into the great river. The discovery of Lake Albert added to the prevailing confusion over the sources of the Nile. Could there be so many?

The couple decided to return to England. Their return journey did not prove easy. The porters deserted them, and the Bakers were able to get away only with Kamrasi's help. In May 1865 they reached Khartoum, and from there they went to Cairo and on to England, where they at last landed after many months.

In 1866 Samuel Baker published an account of his travels, *The Albert Nyanza*. It gives an accurate insight into the author's cast of mind. Observant of the smallest details of the landscape, able to describe any object with vivid precision, Baker had a blind spot when it came to the Africans themselves, and his trip had merely confirmed his preconceived ideas of the

supposedly wild and barbaric character of the peoples of the Great Lakes.

Baker's qualities as an explorer were nonetheless recognized by his contemporaries. He received the gold medal of the Royal Geographical Society before even returning to England, and soon after he was knighted by Queen Victoria.

The Key to the Mystery

All the explorers had come up against the same problem: The topography of the region is so complex that they were unable to gain a picture of the whole. The vast extent of the lakes made it impossible to envision the network of which they form a part. To understand which watercourses feed the lakes and which issue from them required an exploration of their circumferences.

While Speke's theory was beginning to attract a growing number of supporters, there were still questions that needed to be answered. For example, the sources of the White Nile upstream of Lake Victoria had to be precisely located. And was Lake Albert truly the second source of the Nile?

"I hurried to the summit. The glory of our prize burst suddenly upon me! There, like a sea of quicksilver, lay far beneath the grand expanse of water—a boundless sea horizon on the south and southwest. … It is impossible to describe the triumph of that moment; here was the reward for all our labour—for the years of tenacity with which we had toiled through Africa. England had won the sources of the Nile!… I have been permitted to succeed in completing the Nile sources by the discovery of the great reservoir of the equatorial waters, the ALBERT NYANZA, from which the river issues as the entire White Nile."

Samuel Baker
The Albert Nyanza, 1866

In the 1870s David Livingstone and then Henry Morton Stanley attempted in their turn to solve the mystery. The first died without succeeding; his searches were concentrated too far south, in the direction of Lake Tanganyika. Stanley, on the other hand, corroborated Speke's discoveries in May 1875, when he surveyed Ripon Falls and drew the first serious map of Lake Victoria. Stanley, who had already distinguished himself in Africa a few years before by finding Livingstone, later spent several months in the region and established a relationship of mutual respect and trust with the local ruler, King Mutesa. Thanks to the sovereign's help, he was able to discover another stretch of water, Lake Edward, followed by the more modest Lake George. He also saw the famous Mountains of the Moon, the Ruwenzori, whose summits, perpetually covered in snow, are more than sixteen thousand feet above sea level. After many centuries Ptolemy was at last proven right.

The Nile in fact has many sources, as other travelers have proven as recently as the 20th century. The most southerly of them is not far from Lake Tanganyika, and several are situated in Rwanda and Burundi, in east-central Africa. The Nile draws its waters both from the Blue Nile and several branches of the White Nile. One refers, for example, to the Victoria Nile and the Albert Nile. With such complexity, it is scarcely surprising that it has taken so many centuries to trace the sacred river of Egypt to its origins.

The Ruwenzori Mountains, Lake Albert, and Lake Edward, seen from above.

Navigation on Albert Nyanza, a watercolor by explorer Samuel Baker.

"This account is written in the earnest hope that it may contribute to that information which will yet cause the great and fertile continent of Africa to be no longer kept wantonly sealed, but made available as the scene of European enterprise.... Above all, I cherish the hope that it may lead to the introduction of the blessings of the Gospel.**"**

David Livingstone
Missionary Travels, 1857

CHAPTER III
LIVINGSTONE'S MISSION IN SOUTHERN AFRICA

Missionary, ambassador of civilization, explorer: Livingstone played many different roles. It was not easy to work for both Africans and Europeans —their interests so rarely coincided.

By the middle of the 19th century it was the south, rather than the east, of Africa that was best known to Europeans. Drawn there in the 17th century by an agreeable climate, the Dutch had first settled around the Cape. The following century they moved east, attacking the Bantu and robbing them of their lands. In 1806 the British annexed the Cape and sought to impose the abolition of slavery, which was widely practiced by the Dutch Boers. To escape British domination the Boers headed north for the interior. This was the age of the Great Trek (1835–6), in the course of which the Boers settled first in Natal, then in Transvaal and the Orange Free State, all eastern provinces of what is now South Africa.

In This Politically Troubled Atmosphere Livingstone Set Sail

David Livingstone (1813–73) first sailed from England for South Africa in 1840, sent by the London Missionary Society as a medical missionary.

David LIVINGSTONE

Appt. 1840 – Retd. 1857 – Die

Register No. 432

South Africa

Nothing had yet foreshadowed what was to be an exceptional career. Born in Scotland to a poor family, he was obliged to start work at the age of ten in a cotton mill. After a long and grueling working day he pursued his studies at night with passionate dedication. He succeeded in winning a scholarship to the University of Glasgow and went on to receive degrees in medicine and theology.

When he sailed for the African continent at the age of twenty-seven he was convinced he had a sacred mission to teach the Gospel. He reached Kuruman, a town in southern Africa, where the missionary Robert Moffat was already established. The Boers were hostile to the British, however, and did not welcome their missions. After holding out for a few years, Livingstone, who had during this time married Moffat's daughter, Mary, decided to leave Kuruman, which had been razed by the Boers.

The future explorer reacted well to his forced departure. Very independent by nature, he decided to take his wife and children and spread the Gospel in *1873* unexplored regions. The Livingstone family headed north and crossed the vast tract of the Kalahari Desert in a wagon like those used by the Boers on the Great Trek. In July 1849 they reached swamplands that contrasted sharply with the desert they had just crossed.

"At the age of ten I was put into the factory as a 'piecer,'" Livingstone wrote in *Missionary Travels* (1857). The factory was at Blantyre (below). He worked there from 6 AM to 8 PM, and then went to evening classes until 10 PM, after which he studied until midnight.

"I embarked for Africa in 1840, and, after a voyage of three months, reached Cape Town [below].... I started for the interior by going round to Algoa Bay,... and have spent the following sixteen years of my life...in medical and missionary labours there...."

On 1 August 1849 Livingstone became the first European to set eyes on Lake Ngami (northwest Botswana), which earned him an award from the Royal Geographical Society.

Fired by his success as an amateur explorer, Livingstone decided to become a professional and set himself the goal of mastering astronomical calculations. Then, in 1851, he embarked on a series of expeditions that made his tour of Lake Ngami seem a tame family outing.

He lived first among the Makololo on the middle reaches of the Zambezi River. Their chief, Sebituane, was remarkably helpful. Livingstone took the opportunity to travel all over the region, getting as far as Sesheke in June 1851.

Anticipating Danger, He Sent His Family Back to England

His family was still with him at this point, and Mary was pregnant. The baby would be the fourth born to the couple in Africa. One of their children had died in infancy on one of their moves, and another was sick with a fever. Conscious of the dangers to which he was exposing his family and also, no doubt, of the constraints they placed on him, Livingstone accompanied them to Cape Town, from where they made their way back to England. This decision amply illustrates the extent of his ambition. He sacrificed his family life to his African objectives— a decision that may not, perhaps, have suited those he left behind.

Now free to undertake the most arduous of expeditions, he decided to try to find a route that would link the Zambezi to the west coast, while avoiding Boer

Joseph Thomson (left) explored the area between the Zambezi and the Great Lakes from 1879 to 1890, a period of transition, after the great discoveries and before the colonial influx. A trained geologist, he is noted more for his method than his discoveries, though he traveled over three thousand miles. He was tireless but considerate of his men and always tried to pursue his journeys peacefully, avoiding trouble.

territories. The projected journey covered more than a thousand miles.

The First Journey Across the Continent: From the Zambezi to the West Coast

Livingstone first went to Linyanti (in today's Namibia), the Makololo capital. The new chief, Sekeletu, was friendly and eager to further his own business interests. He helped the explorer get a small expedition underway.

The party comprised a modest total of twenty-seven men. In addition to supplies and weapons, Livingstone took with him a range of instruments: a sextant, a thermometer, a compass, a telescope, and even a magic lantern to show scenes from the Holy Bible. The expedition left Linyanti in 1853 and headed northwest. Initially the group advanced by boat, a particularly

Livingstone arriving at Lake Ngami with his family (above). "Twelve days after our departure from the wagons at Ngabisane we came to the northeast end of Lake Ngami; and on the 1st of August, 1849, we went down together to the broad part, and, for the first time, this fine-looking sheet of water was beheld by Europeans.... It is shallow...[and] can never, therefore, be of much value as a commercial highway."

practical form of transport, given that Livingstone suffered from malaria. Despite his illness, at every stop Livingstone recorded a host of details and observations in his diary, a practice that proved invaluable when he later came to write an account of his travels. He was interested in the flora of Africa and noted all the information he could gather on medicinal plants, using himself as a guinea pig.

When navigation became impossible, Livingstone traveled on the back of an ox. Progress through the dense tropical vegetation was difficult, and the heat stifling. To make matters worse, relations with the Africans in the

"Nobody knows whence it comes and whither it goes," says an African canoe song recorded by Livingstone, who observed: "The river itself is, to them, mysterious." Rapids and waterfalls indeed make it difficult to go up the Zambezi, which covers about 1700 miles from Angola to the Indian Ocean. The watercolor below is of the explorer's launch, the *Ma Robert*.

territories he crossed on occasion proved tense; there was mutual mistrust, and heavy tributes were exacted.

After Months En Route Livingstone Reached Luanda, Capital of Angola

On 31 May 1854 the expedition at last reached the Atlantic Ocean. The explorer was utterly exhausted, and he and his men spent three months in the Portuguese colony, then known as São Paulo de Loanda, recuperating. Livingstone put his time to good use by writing a report for the Royal Geographical Society—and then he decided to make his way back to the Zambezi by the same route.

If Livingstone's only declared aim was to open up the continent, he was nonetheless not indifferent to fame. For his return trip he refused to be accompanied

This fragment of Livingstone's journal (top) demonstrates the shortages he endured by his policy of traveling light. Paper was a rare commodity, and he needed plenty of it to keep his extensive and regular records, describe landscapes and routes, and take topographical measurements, for which the sextant (above) proved useful. Memory could not be relied upon amid the fatigues of travel. The explorer also reckoned that if any mishap befell him, his companions could give his papers to the next white man they met.

by a German-Portuguese naturalist on the grounds that the presence of another European would steal some of the glory that his discoveries would bring him. By the time he returned to Linyanti, the medical missionary had covered almost 2500 miles.

While his expedition had deepened his knowledge of Africa and enabled him to chart the regions he had crossed, Livingstone realized that the path he had taken was too difficult and too long to become an established route to the interior.

He was not satisfied: His goal was to open a path along which Christianity and European trade could penetrate to the heart of the continent.

Livingstone Tried His Luck to the East

So in September 1855 he again set forth, this time heading east. And it was again Sekeletu who took charge of organizing the expedition. He provided the missionary with a large quantity of ivory to enable him to pay the tributes that would be exacted from him along the way.

Livingstone set out to follow the Zambezi downstream. On 17 November 1855 he came upon waterfalls producing so much spray that they were visible more

"After twenty minutes' sail from Kalai, we came in sight, for the first time, of the columns of vapour, appropriately called 'smoke.'... Five columns now arose, and bending in the direction of the wind, they seemed placed against a low ridge covered with trees; the tops of the columns at this distance appeared to mingle with the clouds. They were white below, and higher up became dark, so as to simulate smoke very closely. The whole scene was extremely beautiful; the banks and islands dotted over the river are adorned with sylvan vegetation of great variety."

David Livingstone
Missionary Travels, 1857

than five miles away and could even be mistaken for a fire. This was the "smoke that thunders," which he named Victoria Falls. It was a magnificent sight. To mark the excitement of his discovery the missionary engraved his initials on the trunk of a tree. He then pressed on, crossing a deserted region devastated by wars and the raids of the slave traders. He was forced to pay high tributes, and he endured much hostility—a result of the slave traffic. Livingstone's party made long detours to avoid some of the villages.

By the time he got to the Portuguese trading station of Tete in Mozambique, Livingstone had exhausted his strength and had to be carried on a litter. In May 1856 he reached Quelimane, on the Indian Ocean, becoming the first European to cross the African continent. Unfortunately, the route he had followed eastward proved scarcely more viable than the one he had found for his earlier westward journey, but his experiences increased knowledge of the area to a remarkable degree.

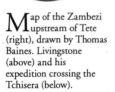

Map of the Zambezi upstream of Tete (right), drawn by Thomas Baines. Livingstone (above) and his expedition crossing the Tchisera (below).

Back in London the Explorer Was Accorded the Highest Honors

Livingstone's fame matched his achievements as a traveler. When he returned to England in 1856 it was

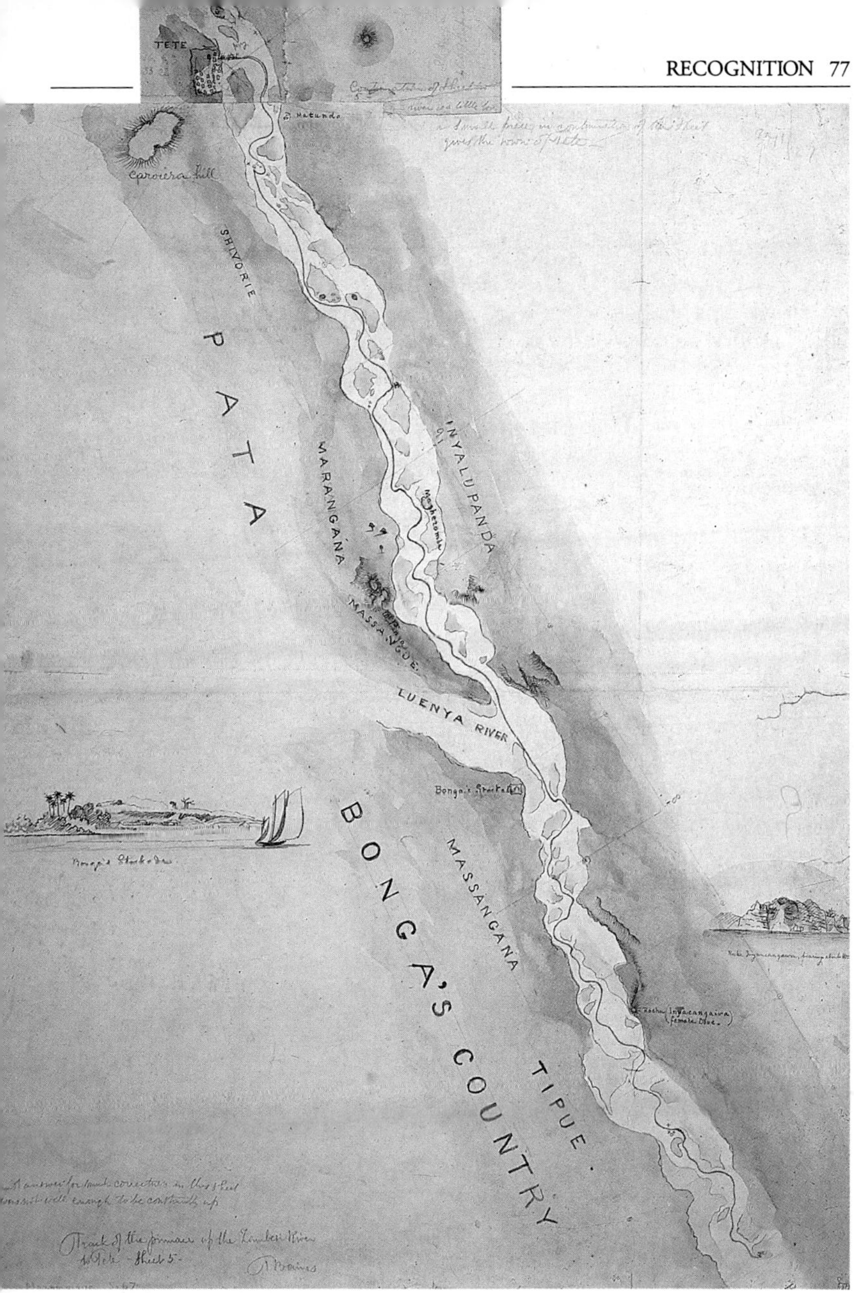
TETE
SHIVORIE
PATA
INYALUPANDA
MARANGANA
MASSANGUE
LUENYA RIVER
Bonga's Stockade
BONGA'S COUNTRY
MASSANGANA
TIPUE

with the intention of making his experiences known and persuading his compatriots to go to Africa and spread "civilization." He was given an overwhelming reception. Raised to the status of national hero, he was asked to give talks to scientific societies, universities, and other influential institutions, invited to attend official dinners, and given many honors and medals.

His worldly triumphs did not stop him from writing an account of his voyages: *Missionary Travels* (1857). It was an instant success and became a best-seller, with over seventy thousand copies sold. The book apppealed to a wide range of readers: armchair travelers eager for tales of adventure, geographers wishing to fill gaps in their knowledge of the "Dark Continent," missionaries drawn by pagan lands, merchants dreaming of new markets, and humanists horrified by the pages devoted to the traffic in slaves.

Livingstone and the Slave Trade

The explorer had traveled through regions where the traffic in slaves was rampant. While the official policy of repression was enforced by the British in West Africa, trade was widespread throughout the rest of the continent. Like many of his contemporaries, Livingstone was firmly convinced that a European presence would guarantee an end to this disgraceful activity. The reality, however, proved more complex. Though the slave traffic was at this period essentially carried on by

Thomas Baines, a member of Livingstone's 1858 expedition, painted marvelous watercolors of the southern African landscape. His subject above is the basin of the Zambezi.

Arabs on the east coast and a few ethnic groups in Central Africa, some whites were at the very least accomplices. Among them were the Portuguese, who were particularly concentrated in the ports of the East African coast and Angola.

In any event, Livingstone's descriptions profoundly affected his contemporaries. He told of long caravans of captives in chains, whipped when they dragged behind and beaten when they could no longer keep up. Travelers to Central Africa were unable to avoid the subject, as they often had to use the same routes as the slave traders. Concerned by the extent of the problem, Livingstone made it his main reason for returning to Africa.

Livingstone fiercely denounced the conniving of the authorities in the slave trade. He reported: "Fifty more slaves were freed next day.... The head of this gang, whom we knew as the agent of one of the principal merchants of Tete, said that they had the licence of the Governor for all they did...."

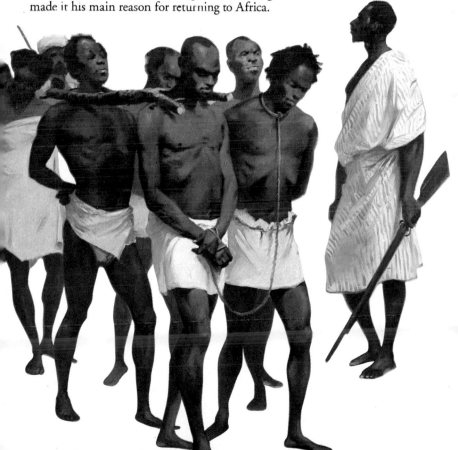

The Explorer Returned to Africa with the Government and Public Opinion Behind Him

Though his period in London wearied him, Livingstone profited nonetheless from his sudden celebrity. Having promoted the explorer to the rank of consul, the Foreign Office assigned him a series of precise tasks, one of which was to establish a station on the Zambezi that would serve as a base for the "civilizing mission" of Great Britain. Livingstone welcomed his new backers, because he had lost the support of the London Missionary Society, which had criticized him for carrying out his missionary work in too sporadic a fashion—a price he paid for his success as an explorer.

This time Livingstone did not set out alone. He sailed for Africa in 1858 with six companions, among them

his brother and the painter Thomas Baines. The size and methodical organization of this expedition were in marked contrast to his previous, poorly financed ventures. The seven British men were accompanied by some sixty porters.

In the course of this expedition Livingstone and his fellow explorers discovered Lake Nyasa (now Lake Malawi), which covers 11,430 square miles. The

M ary Livingstone (left) traveled from England to join her husband on the Zambezi. Though well accustomed to Africa and blessed with a strong constitution, she succumbed to fever, and the expedition doctor was powerless to save her. She died in April 1862 and was buried at the foot of a baobab tree (above left).

Portuguese had heard tales of its existence but never seen it. The British team also investigated the courses of two new rivers, the Shire and the Ruvuma.

Overall, however, this well-planned expedition was a failure. The Zambezi proved to be unnavigable, and no permanent Christian missions were established. To make matters worse, Livingstone, who was highly effective as a lone explorer, showed himself ill equipped to manage a team.

In 1863 he was summoned back to Great Britain, where he stayed only long enough to write a second book: *The Zambezi and Its Tributaries*. Its success was assured before publication. He was again impatient to

This painting of Livingstone's launch, the *Ma Robert,* is by Thomas Baines. The small, twelve-ton steamboat was specially designed for the 1858 expedition and could carry thirty-six passengers. However, it proved prone to rust, consumed enormous quantities of wood, and advanced very slowly— and was soon renamed the *Asthmatic.*

The historic meeting between Stanley (below) and Livingstone. Stanley described the occasion (left): "I would have run to him, only I was a coward in the presence of such a mob—would have embraced him, only, he being an Englishman, I did not know how he would receive me; so I did what cowardice and false pride suggested was the best thing—walked deliberately to him, took off my hat, and said..."

resume his travels, fascinated by the opposing views of Speke and Burton on the source of the Nile.

The Third Expedition in the Region of Lake Tanganyika

Livingstone again obtained financial backing from the Foreign Office, supplemented by the Royal Geographical Society. Abandoning the more southerly areas, the explorer landed at the mouth of

the Ruvuma in January 1866 and headed northwest as
far as Lake Nyasa and Lake Tanganyika. He discovered
Lake Mweru and its effluent, the Lualaba River, which
he took to be the Nile. (He believed the Lualaba's source
was Lake Bangweulu, south of Lake Mweru.) He was
meanwhile laid low with sickness, and his medicine chest
had disappeared. Infirm and incapable of verifying his
topographical hypotheses, he had himself transported to
Ujiji, on Lake Tanganyika. He made attempts to explore
the Lualaba region, and wanted to follow its course
downstream. But the Arab traders at the Nyangwe (in
today's Zaire) station prevented him, and Livingstone
was obliged to return to Ujiji.

Dr. Livingstone, I Presume?

By 1871 Europe had been without news of the explorer
for three years. Some of his porters, returning
prematurely to the coast, had spread rumors of his death.
But the Europeans were not wholly convinced.

As it happened, Livingstone was not "lost"; he knew
exactly where he was, and he had excellent guides with
him, namely Susi, Chuma, and Jacob Wainwright, who
had accompanied him for years. But he was of necessity
heavily reliant on the Arab traders who regularly plied
the route between Ujiji and the coast, and his strong
opposition to the slave traffic did little to win him the
sympathies of those who were engaged in it. The Arab
traders were not in the least anxious to help him
maintain his contacts with Europe, and they balked at
acting as his messengers.

Then, on 30 October 1871, there was great
commotion at Ujiji. Susi came to report that a white
man was about to land. This was Henry Morton Stanley,
(1841–1904) who had set out a few months earlier in
search of the missing doctor and explorer. An American
journalist who had been born in Wales, Stanley was sent
to Africa by the proprietor of the New York *Herald,*
James Gordon Bennett. Bennett was convinced that
Livingstone was still alive and trusted to Stanley's
tenacity to pursue his quest to its conclusion. His
success would bring the paper unprecedented publicity.

Bennett's intuition proved well founded, and the

Stanley's caravan
(above). He and
Livingstone were
diametrically opposed in
their exploring styles.
Stanley was a natural
leader at the head of a
huge caravan, which
included women and
children. Livingstone,
more modest but no
less effective, was a
solitary traveler.

now-legendary meeting of the two men took place in the settlement on the shores of Lake Tanganyika. Hardly able to conceal his emotion and joy, Stanley, face to face with Livingstone, uttered those words whose very banality, given the significance of the occasion, have made them famous: "Dr. Livingstone, I presume?" "Yes," replied the missionary with equal coolness.

Stanley delivered him some letters and medicine, and he even opened a bottle of champagne to mark the occasion in a fitting manner.

In his search for Livingstone, Stanley, accompanied by 190 people, had covered over two thousand miles in 411 days. It has to be said that, unlike other explorers, he had the benefit of extremely generous financial backing. Bennett had pressed £1000 upon him on his departure and told him the funds would be replenished as often as necessary. A few minutes before their historic encounter, the scale of Stanley's expedition had led Livingstone, noting the approaching party, to remark: "This must be a luxurious traveler, and not one at his wits' end like me."

A Last Journey Across the Continent

Despite their differences of character, the two men were instantly drawn to each other, and they set out together on a month's circumnavigation of Lake Tanganyika. A crew of sixteen rowers was hired for the trip. Like Burton, they established that the Ruzizi flowed into the lake rather than out of it. And they were forced to admit that it could not be the Nile.

Resisting the admonitions of Stanley, who saw that he was in a very weak state, Livingstone refused to return to England. He left the journalist at Kazeh in March 1872 to continue his search for the source of the Nile.

He went first to the area around Lake Bangweulu (northern Zambia). It was the middle of the rainy season, and what little strength he had left seeped away. He lost his bearings and his way, had great difficulty eating, and suffered repeated hemorrhages. He was

At the mouth of the Ruzizi: "Myriad channels, rushing by isolated clumps of sedge and matete grass."

Livingstone's last entries in his journal (above) are deeply moving. Utterly worn out, he could only summon up a sentence or two. "I am excessively weak," the missionary wrote on 20 April 1873. The next day: "Tried to ride, but was forced to lie down, and they carried me back to vil. exhausted." The next week all he noted each day was the date. He died on 1 May.

Left: Livingstone and his porters cross a flooded river.

convinced that the Lualaba, which started as the Congo, was one with the Nile—a conviction that developed into an obsession.

Livingstone was never to know that he was in fact mistaken. On the morning of 1 May 1873, in a small village in what is now Zambia, his African companions found him dead, kneeling at the foot of his bed. They embalmed his corpse with salt and alcohol and carried it to Zanzibar: its last voyage across African soil. Thus Great Britain was able to give Livingstone the state funeral that befitted a national hero. Livingstone was buried in Westminster Abbey in London in April 1874.

Livingstone's Posthumous Fame

Contrary to legend, other white men had preceded Livingstone in some of the regions he was thought to have discovered. A number of Portuguese explorers had visited the banks of the Zambezi as early as the start of the 16th century. But this in no way diminishes Livingstone's importance: He remains one of the great explorers of all time.

While his exploits are outstanding, the reasons for his great renown need to be examined. The studies that have been made of Livingstone's life and work are often closer to hagiography than to historical analysis; they stress how he worked ceaselessly for the good of the Africans, refused to use force, and treated his bearers and servants with generosity and kindness. He was certainly not a violent man, but his peaceable character has been exaggerated by claims that he refused to make use of a gun, even for hunting.

He undoubtedly paid the Africans great respect, yet his vision was still colored by his belief in the superiority of the white man, a superiority he regarded not as innate, but the result of education and the influence of Christianity. His celebrity can also be explained

Livingstone died in a small village. His men were deeply moved by his death, and the position in which they found his body made a great impression on them.

Livingstone's body reached Zanzibar in February 1874 and was handed over with his papers and possessions to a Mr. Arthur Laing. On 16 April it arrived in Southampton on the *Malwa*. Taken next to London, the body was examined by Sir William Fergusson and Livingstone's friends. The faulty articulation of the left arm left no doubt of its identity: Livingstone had been bitten by a lion in 1843, which crushed his humerus at the shoulder. This popular 19th-century print (left) is based on the incident.

Faithful retainer Jacob Wainwright (below) guards the body and belongings of his deceased master in Zanzibar.

by the fact that he flattered the self-esteem of the English and of Europeans generally. A humble hero, he devoted himself wholly to the Africans he had come to "save," and to the Europeans whom he encouraged to carry on his mission.

Livingstone spent nearly thirty years traveling in a region little known to the outside world and then died there, as he himself had wished. And though he lost his health, his family, and his hopes of the instant redemption of Africa, he contributed extensively to European knowledge of the continent—for better or worse.

LIVINGSTON N°1

" Livingstone called floating down the Lualaba a foolhardy feat. So it is, and were I to do it again, I would not attempt [it] without two hundred guns.... I pen these lines with half a feeling that they will never be read by any other white person; still, as I persist in continuing the journey, I persist in writing, leaving events and their disposal to an All-Wise Providence. **"**

The Exploration Diaries of Henry Morton Stanley

CHAPTER IV
INTO THE HEART OF THE FOREST

In the late 19th century all European eyes focused on the Congo, and colonial claims were settled by joint agreements. The Berlin Conference (1884–5) set out the basis of colonization, notably in the Congo. Left: The British and French met in 1899.

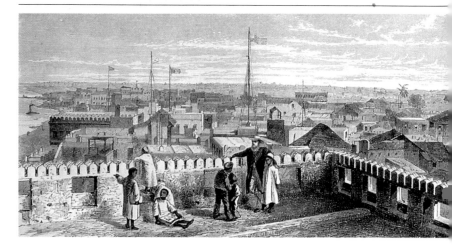

Until the 1870s geographical research was limited to the area around the Great Lakes and to southern Africa. There remained one great unknown: the Congo basin, the kingdom of the great equatorial forest. Even though it was particularly difficult to penetrate—for both political and topographical reasons—within a few years the Congo had nonetheless become a major stake in the power games of the various European colonizing powers. Here, more than anywhere else, the links between exploration and imperialism are apparent.

In the Footsteps of Livingstone: Cameron Crossed the Dark Continent

Just at the time when Stanley found Livingstone, the Royal Geographical Society had been itself planning to send an expedition to Central Africa in search of him.

It was a lieutenant in the Royal Navy, Verney Lovett Cameron (1844–94), who volunteered to lead the venture. He had previously served on a vessel engaged in the repression of the slave traffic in the region of Zanzibar. The son of a minister, he was convinced of the need for a European presence in Africa.

Although he had no references to support his candidature, the Royal Geographical Society was won over by Cameron's determination and put him in charge

Zanzibar, a small island off the east coast of Africa, experienced an economic boom in the 19th century and became one of the main African trading centers. It was a great slave market and also handled large quantities of ivory, much in demand among the European bourgeoisie. Arabs and Indians running prosperous businesses helped the explorers organize their expeditions by supplying them with goods and labor.

Verney Lovett Cameron (below) crossed territories already known to Portuguese slave traders in 1875, but he was the first to record observations on their river networks, botany, and ethnography. The expedition took place in the rainy season, which made progress even more difficult. Nonetheless, only two people died in the thirty-one months en route. This illustration (left) is of the Cameron expedition crossing the Lovoi River.

of the expedition. In January 1873 Cameron landed in Zanzibar and spent several weeks there organizing a caravan, which consisted of the very considerable number of two hundred porters. Very soon, however, there were desertions: Having found it difficult to recruit men, Cameron had made the serious error of paying them before they started.

On 23 March 1873 he left Bagamoyo with his baggage train, accompanied by two other Britons, Dr. W. E. Dillon and Cecil Murphy. From the very beginning the caravan had difficulty getting supplies. The price of food and the tolls exacted along the way were exorbitant, and the team's stock of cloth and shells to be used for barter was quickly exhausted. The Europeans were seriously afflicted by malaria. A nephew of Livingstone's, Robert Moffat, who had joined the party in Natal, fell victim to the disease in May. Despite the hardships, the expedition continued on its route—the very one that had been followed ten years earlier by Burton and Speke.

In October Cameron Received Painful News: The Man He Was Looking for Was Dead

In Kazeh Cameron met Livingstone's porters on their way to Zanzibar carrying the missionary's body. The expedition's main objective was thus frustrated, and Cameron had to decide what to do next. Murphy and Dillon chose to go back, leaving their companion to continue his journey alone.

Cameron reached Ujiji on 18 February 1874 and recovered Livingstone's personal papers from an Arab trader. It was his privilege to bear these back to Great Britain—some small consolation at least.

Cameron's dream was to explore the area west of Lake Tanganyika, but he was strongly advised to wait a few months. The region was unsafe, he was told, and he would need to travel with a large caravan, which he no longer had. He therefore turned his attention to the southern shores of the lake and explored them for two months, measuring the altitude and charting some five hundred miles. Cameron's discovery was that in the rainy season the lake released its waters into the Lukuga, a river forming part of the Congo drainage system.

Cameron Headed South Instead of Descending the Course of the River

He now turned west and resolved to track the course of the Lualaba. But when he reached Nyangwe in August 1874, the Arab trader Tippu Tib persuaded him to abandon the venture as reckless. The explorer was to regret his failure to persevere when Stanley won fame doing so three years later.

In any case, Cameron was at least in a position to

A river's name often changed during its course, to the confusion of Europeans. The Congo was known as the Lualaba in the east—and then Stanley complicated matters by calling it the Livingstone. Above: The upper Zambezi.

Cameron and many of his compatriots believed that only the British were capable of putting an end to the slave trade (right), thus justifying their presence in Africa.

confirm that the Lualaba and the Nile could not be the same river. The altitude of the Lualaba at Nyangwe was lower than that of the Nile at Gondokoro, and its volume five times as great.

Following Tippu Tib's advice, Cameron headed south, aiming to cross the continent in a westerly direction. The ordeals the explorer endured were evidence of the rashness of his undertaking. The expedition was plagued by constant famine, he suffered from scurvy, and relations with the local people were extremely tense.

Whatever his qualms, Cameron and his retinue were obliged to travel part of the route in the company of a slave merchant.

Tippu Tib (above) was the most powerful merchant in central Africa. Very independent of the sultan of Zanzibar, he operated around Nyangwe, sending his men to scour the region for ivory and slaves.

On 7 November 1875 Cameron finally reached Benguela on the coast of Angola, completing his journey across the continent; he was the first European to cross equatorial Africa. His men were in such a state of exhaustion that he had to leave most of them behind while he and a few faithful followers went ahead to obtain help from the Portuguese on the coast.

When he landed in Liverpool in 1876 Cameron was accorded an ecstatic reception by the scientific world. The Royal Geographical Society gave him an award, and he received a number of honorary titles from distinguished universities and from Queen Victoria in person.

The expedition had cost the considerable sum of £12,000, which obliged the RGS to appeal for private contributions. On the urging of his friends, Cameron published an account of his adventures, *Across Africa* (1877), which reveals his genuine interest in the Africans. His book is also a powerful argument against the slave trade, whose cruelties he had been obliged to witness firsthand.

It is curious that Cameron is not as famous as other explorers, for his achievements are no less remarkable, and the European powers were very quick to interest themselves in the regions he had discovered. His neglect by posterity is perhaps due partly to Cameron's own reticence, but he has above all been overshadowed by the towering figure of Stanley, who followed him.

Stanley Nursed a Wild Ambition to Go Down the Lualaba, in the Belief that It Was the Congo

Having already earned his reputation by finding Livingstone, Henry Morton Stanley had no trouble in obtaining the backing he needed for his next great project: to go down the Lualaba. Financed by two newspaper magnates, the proprietors of the New York *Herald* and the London *Daily Telegraph*, he organized a massive expedition. It included the *Lady Alice*, a forty-foot boat which he took with him in sections, and a retinue of 360 men, including three Europeans: the brothers Frank and Edward Pocock, and Frederick Barker.

This engraving is of the young Stanley. Born John Rowlands in Wales in 1841, the illegitimate son of a servant, he went to work at the age of fourteen as a cabin boy on a ship headed for America. There he was adopted by a trader, whose name he assumed. In 1865 he became a journalist and covered a story on Abyssinia (Ethiopia) for the New York *Herald,* going on to win legendary fame as the man who found Livingstone.

Setting out from Zanzibar on 17 November 1874, Stanley stopped near the Great Lakes. He then headed northwest and reached Nyangwe in October 1876. Only one European, Frank Pocock, was still with him; the others had died on the way. Downstream of the Nyangwe station the great forest began, humid and thickly overgrown. Stanley's venture seemed increasingly hazardous, and he decided to toss a coin to determine whether or not to go on: The coin indicated he should

To Stanley's great grief, the three Europeans (pictured below) on his expedition did not survive the journey to reach the Atlantic. The dogs also perished. From left to right: Frank Pocock, Frederick Barker, a boy from Zanzibar, Edward Pocock, and Kalulu.

A carpenter in Zanzibar was given the task of cutting the *Lady Alice* into the sections shown here being transported. The original intention had been to carry the boat in one piece. Stanley named the *Lady Alice* after his betrothed, but by the time he returned from his expedition, Alice had married someone else.

retrace his steps. Exasperated, Stanley defied superstition and pressed ahead.

Having found Tippu Tib to be a staunch ally, Stanley made a deal with him. In exchange for $5000 Tippu Tib provided Stanley with an escort of seven hundred men for a period of two months, as well as food and extra weapons.

On 5 November 1876 the column of men set off north along the river. For days their boats made their way down its waters. The air was unhealthy, the vegetation extremely dense, and the peoples living on the banks were reputed to be cannibals and easily provoked. The travelers did not always find a friendly welcome, their presence being regarded as a threat. In some places Stanley sowed terror by an excessive use of firearms. He lost men in ambushes and responded by razing whole villages. The explorer was involved in thirty-two battles on this expedition.

Stanley Falls and Stanley Pool

The river made its way north for hundreds of miles. Was it truly the Congo, as Stanley thought? His belief was confirmed when, near the equator, the river turned west,

Arthur Jephson (above) joined Stanley's last expedition in 1887. Right: Frank Pocock's death in the rapids. To the Africans, the arrival of a caravan often meant a slave raid. This explains at least some of their hostility to Europeans, seen in the illustration below. Some Africans also believed the whites to be cannibals.

and in January 1877 he found the gigantic waterfalls that he modestly named after himself. In February Stanley learned from an African chief that the river was called the Congo. There was no more room for doubt.

But the expedition had alas only covered half of the route. The cataracts were an obstacle to further progress, and a number of men drowned in the rapids. In March the survivors finally reached a large lake, which was immediately christened Stanley Pool.

It was a full five months later that the party drew near the ocean. Their arrival was traumatic. Half the men had died, and Stanley himself seemed crushed by what he had endured. In his journal he complained of exhaustion and, even more, of the intense lassitude that had come over him.

The Africans on the Atlantic shore were impossible to trade with, as they had little interest in the merchandise that the expedition was offering. In addition, Stanley's porters stole food in the villages, which did nothing to improve relations with the native population.

On 4 August 1877, at the

end of his tether, Stanley sent a group of scouts for help. The expedition was rescued, but men nonetheless continued to die of exhaustion. The survivors longed to return home, which further weakened morale, so Stanley sent them back to Zanzibar by boat. He himself had aged considerably. His hair had turned white, and he looked somber and had grown terribly thin.

This was hardly surprising. The journey had lasted a thousand days in horrific conditions, as recounted by Stanley in his book *Through the Dark Continent* (1878). The expedition has gone down in history as the most dramatic of all those to have taken place in Africa.

On his return to England Stanley married a rich heiress descended from Oliver Cromwell. The match was not welcomed by the upper classes, who looked askance at this adventurer and were not pleased to see him join their ranks.

In the Following Years the Journalist Continued His African Career

At the end of the 1870s Stanley entered the service of Belgian King Leopold II, who in 1876 had founded the Association Internationale Africaine and dreamed of expanding his influence overseas. With Stanley's help Leopold II was able to carve himself a personal empire on the left bank of the Congo.

Stanley, full of plans for the exploitation of the basin, hoped in particular to open a route that would bypass the cataracts. He also started the building of a railway and founded Leopoldville, on Stanley Pool, and Stanleyville, revealing a partiality for his own name that verges on a personality cult. To establish a power base for Leopold, he had to persuade certain African chiefs to accept the king's protection.

The scale of the work Stanley carried out in the Congo between 1879 and 1884 quickly earned him the nickname *Boula Matari*, "Breaker of Stones." His efforts could hardly, however, be described as disinterested. The riches of the interior were such that in the course of his 1876 expedition Stanley collected ivory that he sold for over $50,000.

Stanley led a final expedition to Africa in 1887–9. He set out to rescue a German explorer by the name of Mehmed Emin Pasha, who was the governor of an Egyptian province in the Sudan and had been cut off by a Mahdist revolt not far from Lake Albert. This time the caravan numbered over eight hundred men when it left Zanzibar.

It was in truth a strange expedition, for when, after months of forced march and hunger, Emin Pasha was finally found, he no longer wanted to leave. Stanley

This advertisement appeared in 1900. The regime established in the Belgian Congo by Leopold II (left) was soon decried for its extreme brutality. Emin Pasha's 1890 expedition (below).

Leopoldville (today's Kinshasa, seen here in an 1888 painting by Frans Hens) was an archetypal colonial town. It was founded in 1881 on the site of an earlier settlement, Kintambo, and was named after Leopold II by Stanley. Not until 1926 did it become the capital of the Belgian Congo, having initially been envisaged as an outpost of civilization on the left bank of the river. Stanley also founded Stanleyville in 1883, immediately below Stanley Falls. No one was going to be allowed to forget the name of the man who opened up the Congo.

had to persuade him to allow himself to be liberated.

This was Stanley's last adventure, recounted in his book *In Darkest Africa* (1890). After this he settled in Surrey, England, where he spent his remaining years enjoying his literary success and tasting, more or less happily, the joys of married life.

Savorgnan de Brazza, Representative of France

When he plunged into colonial conquest in the early 1880s, Stanley found himself confronted with the ambitions of the French, represented in the area by Pierre Savorgnan de Brazza (1852–1905). Brazza, born an Italian count, had served as a lieutenant in the French navy even before he became a naturalized French citizen in 1874.

Thanks to the navy minister, who was a friend of his, he was put in charge of a reconnaissance trip to the Ogooué River (Gabon). The French, who had had a settlement at the mouth of the river since 1842, were ill acquainted with its upper reaches.

Only a somewhat eccentric French-

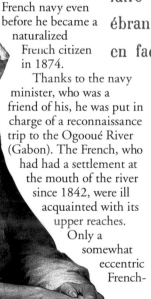

la peau de son front, rejet
en tous sens le poil qui l
une expression diaboliqu
faire trembler la forêt ; i
ébranlait le sol sous me
en face, et se battant la

Above: An excerpt from a French edition of Paul Du Chaillu's *Explorations and Adventures in Equatorial Africa*.

Brazza's colonial mission on behalf of France was as costly as it was ambitious. He received a grant of 17,500 francs for his first expedition to the Ogooué but spent 40,000—and it was not even a large-scale operation like Stanley's. This portrait of Brazza (left) is dated 1886.

American, Paul Du Chaillu (1831–1903), had traveled in central Africa in the late 1850s. After staying among the Fan, who were reputed cannibals, he had written an account of his experiences of gorilla hunting and had brought back the first gorillas to be seen in America.

Brazza's modest expedition set out in 1875 and lasted two years. He was accompanied by some twenty Africans and three Frenchmen—a doctor, a soldier, and a naturalist, who provided three complementary skills. Brazza and his men successfully ascended the Ogooué, establishing that the river

Stanley (above left), photographed with his wife. His boastfulness and rough manner, as well as his American background, antagonized the English.

n avant et en arrière, faisait mouvoir

recouvrait, et donnait à ses traits

Il poussa encore un rugissement à

me sembla qu'un coup de tonnerre

pieds ; puis le monstre nous regarda

poitrine, avança encore.

could not, as had been hoped, provide a satisfactory means of access to the interior. When it ceased to be navigable, the party headed toward the Alima, a tributary of the Congo, only to be stopped by a group of natives on the riverbank. Rather than engage in a trial of strength, Brazza chose to retrace his steps. This laudable restraint prevented him from reaching the Congo, where Stanley was soon to win fame.

In 1880, having heard of Stanley's explorations, he persuaded the French government to get politically involved in the region. He believed strongly in the civilizing mission of his adopted country, particularly where the slave trade was concerned, and had little respect for Stanley or for the English in general.

Again heading a small band of men, Brazza ascended the Ogooué and reached the north bank of the Congo at the level of Stanley Pool. The region was inhabited by the Bateke and ruled by Makoko, a spiritual as well as

The first descriptions of the gigantic, almost human, gorilla were met with disbelief. Paul Du Chaillu described its roar in *Explorations and Adventures in Equatorial Africa* (1861): "The roar of the gorilla is the most singular and awful noise heard in these African woods. It begins with a sharp bark, like an angry dog, then glides into a deep bass roll, which literally and closely resembles the roll of distant thunder along the sky."

temporal leader, who gave him a ceremonial welcome. Encouraged by his reception, Brazza made him sign a treaty of "friendship," according to which Makoko placed his lands under French protection. He even ceded full ownership of some territory: the future site of Brazzaville. What the French offered Makoko in exchange was a tricolor flag.

The French statesman Jules Ferry receiving delegates from the colonies in 1892. He promoted expansion, particularly into Africa, and encouraged Brazza to occupy the Congo.

Following a quick meeting with Stanley, Brazza obtained French confirmation of the treaty. Then in 1883 he set forth again with a more constructive mission: to establish stations and carry out surveys of the topography and the peoples in the region of the Ogooué. This time the expedition numbered a hundred men, for France no longer hesitated to invest in the colonial adventure. Brazza was nonetheless summoned back home in 1885. He spent the following years defending his colonial vision: conquest with "a human face." The sincerity of his belief won him tremendous popularity.

An Exceptional Character: Mary Kingsley

In the long list of names of explorers one remarkable woman stands out: Mary Henrietta Kingsley (1862–1900), who set sail for equatorial Africa in 1893. She had two objectives: to bring back specimens of fish for the British Museum and to collect information on African religions. She undertook two voyages, one from July to December 1893 and the other from December 1894 to November 1895.

She explored the coast of Africa by ship from Senegal to Angola. But the region that particularly interested her was present-day Gabon, where she spent a considerable time in 1895. An independent traveler, she was accompanied only by a few porters as she ascended the Ogooué before continuing overland in the direction of Rembwe, to the north, over unmapped territories. Kingsley had no financial support beyond her private means, which were modest. She therefore engaged in trade, offering rum, cloth, and metal fishhooks in exchange for ivory and fish destined for the museum. At the end of her second trip, in 1895, she set out to climb

Mary Kingsley (above) was born in England in 1862 to a doctor and a servant. She did not leave home until she was thirty, her parents having died within months of each other. She taught herself Latin, physics, and chemistry, and she took German classes. Her father, an indefatigable traveler, had given her a taste for distant lands. His library included many travel books and scientific tomes and was a source of considerable interest and information to her.

A statuette from Gabon (left).

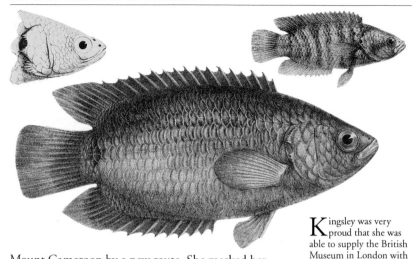

Mount Cameroon by a new route. She marked her arrival at the top in a typically witty fashion, leaving her visiting card under a stone. This sums up that which sets her apart from her male colleagues—a sense of humor and a detachment that make her a particularly delightful character. Her expeditions were brief, but the way she conducted them was unusual. She traveled light, refused to let herself be carried, swam across marshlands, learned to handle a canoe single-handed, slept under the stars, and ate whatever was locally available. Her one luxury was tea.

Kingsley was very proud that she was able to supply the British Museum in London with specimens of then-unknown fish (above), which are now named after her: *Kingsleyae*. She traveled with jars of alcohol (not easy to transport) in which she preserved fish she had caught herself or purchased from African fishermen.

In the Vanguard of Ethnography

An amateur ethnologist, Kingsley spent a period among the Fan people of Gabon and sought to understand their culture in order to protect it better. She studied a number of African customs, such as polygamy, which she defended to the missionaries. Far from passing judgment, she was convinced that every culture has an inner coherence and made efforts to comprehend the bases of African customs—a revolutionary attitude at the time.

By the time she returned to England in 1895 the articles she had published in the press had already made her famous, and her readers were eager for more. She wrote a first book of 750 pages, published in 1897: *Travels in West Africa* (a somewhat misleading title as she had traveled more in equatorial than in West Africa). An instant success, the book was reprinted four times in its first year and followed by a second volume, *West African Studies* (1899). Her writings are primarily ethnographic, and she was quickly acknowledged as an authority on the African world.

Private adviser to the minister for the colonies, Joseph Chamberlain, she met the anthropologist Sir Edward Burnett Tylor and became an intimate of Stanley and Rudyard Kipling, insisting all the time that she had accomplished nothing remarkable. Kingsley succumbed to a tropical disease at the age of thirty-nine in South Africa, where she had gone as a nurse to tend the Boer prisoners taken by the British. A proud imperialist, she fought relentlessly for "intelligent" colonization that would be more accommodating of African customs and correspondingly more effective.

Mary Kingsley, a unique figure in history, enlivened the portrait gallery of 19th-century explorers, showing that a woman could win distinction in these remote lands.

Kingsley took this photograph of a Fan family. She was unusual in working as an ethnologist in the field. Unfortunately, her powers of empirical observation and the conclusions she drew, however well meant, often proved ill founded. The science of anthropology was still in its infancy, and Kingsley was not free of the preconceptions of her time. Among other misapprehensions, she was a firm believer in the polygenist theory that blacks and whites do not belong to the same branch of the human race.

This carved wooden head (left) is of a Fan girl.

Some of the explorers started their careers as casual travelers, only to discover fairly quickly that Africa was no place for amateurs. The success of an expedition depended on the expertise of its leaders and perhaps even more on the caliber of the porters and guides, less well known, but no less remarkable. Everything had to be organized down to the last detail, and careful planning was as valuable as endurance.

CHAPTER V
THE EXPLORER'S PROFESSION

"Life at Zanzibar is a busy one to the intending explorer... each moment of daylight must be employed in the selection and purchase of the various kinds of cloth, beads, and wire, in demand by the different tribes," wrote Stanley. Left: French explorer Lt. Louis Mizon in the Congo. Right: Burton's Arab passport.

This watercolor of the Kiungani mission (left) and this drawing of a slave market (below) are both set in Zanzibar. The well-sited island quickly attracted the interest of the British, who in 1873 persuaded Sultan Bargash to abolish the slave trade. In 1874 Stanley noted with approval that a church had replaced a former slave market.

An Expedition Was Prepared in Two Stages: The First in Europe, the Second in Africa

A spirit of adventure was obviously a prerequisite of any exploration, but it was not enough in itself. A traveler's first step was to obtain abundant information in Europe about the regions he or she intended to visit.

Kingsley, for example, busily combed libraries, read the accounts of her predecessors (Du Chaillu, Savorgnan de Brazza, Stanley), and pored over a variety of atlases to acquaint herself with the geography of the continent.

The explorers also contacted all the authorities who might be able to help them. In most cases they set sail carrying letters of recommendation addressed to Europeans stationed in Africa. This meant that when they arrived they found governors, consuls, and other officials with local knowledge who could give them hospitality and support.

The explorers' first task on reaching Africa was to recruit men for the expedition. Either, like Kingsley, they engaged a few volunteers at a moment's notice, or they relied on a recruitment agent. In Zanzibar the Arabs filled this role.

What Not to Forget

One of the difficulties in preparing the departure of an expedition was knowing what to pack. The lists drawn up by explorers feature an astonishing variety of objects. The medicine chest, a life-saving item handled with the greatest of care, was generally entrusted to a porter of proven reliability.

Apart from quinine (used since the 1860s to give protection against malaria), morphine, ointments, tonics, bandages, and alcohol were taken—supplemented during the journey by local medicinal plants and remedies, when the Europeans were prepared to try

Europeans, who were prone to suffer from the heat, were often carried on litters, as in this illustration (above) from William Hutton's *A Voyage to Africa* (1821). Every expedition worthy of the name was preceded by a flag, a sign of power and a means of being recognized from afar. Livingstone knew at once that it was an American expedition coming toward him. He was greatly relieved not to be meeting the French, as he spoke not a word of their language.

them as a last resort. The camping equipment was remarkably comprehensive; the explorers did not object to roughing it, but even so some of them wanted to sleep in a bed. They generally brought with them tents, awnings, rugs, mattresses, pillows, mosquito nets, and mats. The porters had to make do with rugs alone. Shoes and clothes, however durable, needed frequent replacement (Burton traveled with three trunks). Curiously, given the African climate, flannel was highly prized; it was thought to protect against fever and the sun.

Tools were necessary to cut paths and build emergency bridges, huts, and canoes. Nor should weapons be forgotten. Finally, there were abundant provisions designed to meet every eventuality. Salt, spices, tea, coffee, fish, meat, canned vegetables, oil, sugar, and crackers supplemented the locally obtained game and supplies.

The Most Unexpected Items Were Brought Along

The explorers did not leave their favorite books behind. Kingsley packed a specialized book on fish, while Burton took at least twenty books on a wide range of subjects, and Stanley apparently read Shakespeare on his expedition down the Congo. This volume indeed served a useful purpose one day, when the Africans became suspicious and asked the explorer to burn his journal, which they took to be a magic object. Rather than part with his precious notebook, Stanley instead threw the great playwright's works into the flames. By a lucky chance they looked very similar.

In addition to books, the more talented travelers took drawing materials on their expeditions.

Scientific equipment was packed for use in topographical surveys and orientation.

All the explorers, however modest their origins, were part of an educated elite, as we can see from their interest in books and faith in science. Here are Burton (above) and Baker (below).

A chronometer, portable sundial, rain gauge, compass, sextant, thermometer, telescope, square, sounding line, and more were part of the baggage. The explorer needed to measure latitude, longitude, and water depth. Without these instruments he or she would be utterly helpless.

Lastly, some of the bundles contained goods intended for barter and for the payment of tributes and tolls. The peoples of the interior willingly bought cloth and manufactured articles, such as fishhooks, wire, and firearms. Some shells (cowries) were widely used as currency.

The equipment and supplies carried were of course largely determined by the type of expedition envisaged. Kingsley took very little baggage and only one revolver, which she never used.

The Financing of Expeditions

It is clear from the list of all that the explorers needed to take with them that the financing of an expedition was of critical importance. Bruce relied on his personal wealth when he traveled in Ethiopia, but starting at the end of the 18th century the number of patrons increased, enabling explorers of more humble birth to venture into Africa.

The proliferation of scientific societies, which often commissioned their own expeditions, was of tremendous benefit to explorers. The name of the Royal Geographical Society is forever linked to the discovery of Africa as a result of the support the society gave to the travels of Speke, Livingstone, and Cameron. The society's involvement was made possible by the growth in its income, which rose from £1000 per annum in the

" As regards shoes, the best would be ammunition boots for walking and jack boots for riding. They must be...at least one size too large in England," wrote Burton.

1850s to £8000 per annum in about 1875. A few specialized journals also encouraged exploration by giving grants to explorers.

The contributions of private benefactors were augmented by those of the state. In the 1860s governments began to invest in geographical research through the agency of official ministries, such as the Foreign Office in Britain and the Ministère de la Marine (Navy ministry) in France.

The most advantageous course was in fact to combine a number of backers. Stanley broke a record when he went to "liberate" Emin Pasha: £33,000 had been placed at his disposal, and he used only four-fifths of it. This sum was provided by a wide range of benefactors, among them the Egyptian government (who supplied nearly half the total), several members of the British aristocracy (including a descendant of James Bruce), the Royal Geographical Society, newspaper readers, and industrial and commercial companies.

The cost of transport represented over 25 percent of

Contrasts in scale: Above, a section of Jean-Baptiste Marchand's boat being carried through the bush; below, the gunboat placed at Brazza's disposal.

the total expense. The salaries of the porters were modest (10 percent), but the ocean crossings and river transport were a heavy burden, further increased by payment of tributes, insurance, medical care, telegrams, and the (meager) compensation paid to the families of porters who died on the journey.

A Caravan Was Organized Along Strictly Hierarchical Lines

At the outset the explorers assigned each person a specific place. Not everyone was of equal status; though the European was always the absolute leader, there were a few privileged individuals who shared some of his or her authority.

Thus there was always a second-in-command on an expedition, rarely an African. The organization of the caravan was effectively a microcosm of the world, as seen

Stanley was besieged with applications —even from mediums: "They all knew Africa, were perfectly acclimatized…[would] take me up in balloons or by flying carriages, make us all invisible by their magic arts, or by the 'science of magnetism,' would cause all savages to fall asleep while we might pass…without trouble."

Above: Regent Street in London, c. 1830, first site of the RGS.

The increasing demand for ivory at the start of the 19th century led to a boom in elephant hunting. Ivory was used to make piano keys, billiard balls, and fashionable trinkets for the drawing rooms of the bourgeoisie. Of no local use, ivory nonetheless revolutionized the life of the Chokwe of Angola and the Nyamwezi by giving them a passport to international trade and enabling them to buy guns.

through Western eyes. At the top were the whites, next to them the Arabs, and right at the bottom were the black Africans.

Some Africans were nonetheless given positions of responsibility. The larger caravans numbered dozens, even hundreds, of men. They were divided into small groups, each with a leader who had to account for the others. Africans were often appointed as leaders. Most spoke Swahili and belonged to the strongly Islamic culture of the east coast. All the supposedly subordinate jobs—porter, rower, handyman—were allocated to Africans. But here again there were differentiations.

Some peoples were particularly valued for their skill as porters, for example. There were, in effect, ethnic specializations. The Nyamwezi, who lived between Lake Victoria and Lake Tanganyika, had a reputation as loyal and hard workers. Operating as slave and ivory merchants, they were also well acquainted with the route between Bagamoyo and their territories. Kingsley, for her part, preferred to employ the Galwa, who were reputed to be the best rowers in Gabon.

Captain Marchand was escorted by 150 Senegalese infantrymen, who were very versatile and worked for the French officers as bearers, soldiers, and servants. Prints and postcards, like that of the Marchand expedition below, were a means of promoting the glory of France and the colonial ideal.

Congo Français

Collection J. Audeoud   94. - Passage de la mission Marchand à Loango

The Allocation of the Various Tasks on an Expedition

In regions where sleeping sickness could wipe out pack animals, most of the baggage was carried on men's backs. The porters were therefore very much in the majority, often representing as much as three-quarters of the group. In 1874 Stanley's men each signed an individual contract with him in the presence of witnesses. It stipulated that the employee, who received an advance equivalent to four months' wages, was

Mouna-Sera and Uledi (left) were bearers for Stanley. Uledi accompanied Stanley on three of his expeditions and was captain of the *Lady Alice*. An excellent swimmer, he saved twelve men from drowning, in some cases by throwing himself into the current. In 1874 he was one of twenty-one group leaders on the expedition down the Congo.

to be well treated and nursed in case of illness. In exchange, he undertook to work for Stanley for at least two years. Each porter was given an allotted place in the line, and a specific pack was also assigned to him. This load was nontransferable and weighed between seventy and eighty pounds.

The expedition, however, did not consist entirely of porters. Explorers employed one or two personal servants who were always in close attendance, ready to hand them anything they needed, to carry their gun, or serve their food. These "boys," as they were known—they often were very young—were valued for their devotion, efficiency, and obedience. Those making up the armed escort protecting the leader were generally older.

Cooks were important members of the team, though the travelers constantly complained of the bad food. This was a critical concern, as the morale of the

Stanley, portrayed with his retinue in this 19th-century engraving, engaged Kalulu as his "boy" in 1871, reckoning that he did him a great honor. "I soon found how apt and quick he was to learn, in consequence of which, he was promoted to the rank of personal attendant. Even Selim could not vie with Kalulu in promptness and celerity, or in guessing my wants at the table. His little black eyes were constantly roving over the dishes, studying out the problem of what was further necessary, or had become unnecessary." Kalulu died in 1877 in the rapids to which Stanley gave his name.

expedition members depended greatly on the quality of their food.

Another key figure was the interpreter, on whose skills all communication depended. Burton, with his linguistic gifts, was very much an exception to the explorers' rule; most explorers had little interest in African languages, though they might pick up a few phrases in the course of their travels. Kingsley even went as far as to maintain, with disconcerting naïveté, that the languages of Gabon were all extremely simple.

In East Africa the common language is Swahili, which belongs to the Bantu group. Interpreters could also speak Arabic, and sometimes English—or rather a form of pidgin English, which the British explorers often imitated with a mixture of mischievousness and condescending superiority. Often several interpreters had to work in sequence: One, for instance, would translate from Swahili into Arabic, and the next from Arabic into English (or vice versa). In other regions, Africans who could speak either French or Portuguese were hired.

E xpeditions sometimes stayed in place for several days. Life would become more restful, with time for excursions, scientific studies, obtaining supplies, tending the sick, and writing. This necklace of human bone (below) belonged to Burton.

Capitaine à 29 ans, il expose au Ministre des Affaires Étrangères son vaste et hardi projet de traverser toute l'Afrique avant les Anglais et il en reçoit aussitôt la périlleuse mission.

Après cette expédition qui dure plus de trois ans et que les Anglais avaient déclarée impossible, il plante le premier le drapeau tricolore sur les bords du Nil à Fashóda, s'y établit formidablement et y cultive des légumes et des fleurs.

Il est l'espoir d

Vive Mar

HONNEUR ET P

Devant l'énergique attitude de l'héroïque Marchand, le général anglais s'entend avec lui pour qu'un officier de la mission aille en France aviser le gouvernement.

Les tristes nécessités de la politique l'obligeant à se retirer, il quitte Fashoda la mort dans l'âme, et reçoit les honneurs militaires de *toute* l'armée anglaise.

a France

hand!

Suivi de son intrépide état-major, et de la petite armée de ses fidèles tirailleurs noirs, il traverse les arides déserts et les marécages de la brousse, où, à toute minute, il court les plus grands dangers.

Il voit arriver les Anglais, et il fait serment, avec ses braves compagnons, de mourir à son poste.

...mé chef de bataillon et Commandeur Légion d'Honneur, il est royalement par Ménélick, Empereur d'Abyssinie, couvre d'honneurs et de présents.

En France, il reçoit, partout sur son passage, l'accueil le plus enthousiaste et il est l'objet à Paris, au Cercle Militaire, d'une ovation triomphale.

The story of Jean-Baptiste Marchand and the Fashoda crisis is told in these popular French prints. Marchand was a French hero at the turn of the century. He was put in charge of an expedition from the Congo to the Nile, the object of which was to establish a French east-west axis from Dakar to Djibouti, linking the Atlantic to the Red Sea. In 1896 Captain Marchand led an enormous party toward the upper Nile, ruthlessly repressing (or, as he called it, "pacifying") anti-French rebellions as he progressed. In July 1898 the expedition reached the Sudanese settlement of Fashoda (today Kodok). No sooner had the French flag been raised than twenty thousand Anglo-Egyptians led by Lord Horatio Kitchener arrived. A grave diplomatic crisis ensued. In November France at last ordered Marchand to withdraw. Though humiliated, French nationalists succeeded in turning the affair into an occasion for fervently patriotic propaganda.

The Africans Played an Essential Role in the "Discovery" of Their Continent

The contribution of the Africans to the "discoveries" can never be sufficiently stressed. Who now remembers Chuma, Susi, Bombay, Uledi, and so many others? Their names have sunk into oblivion, but the courage they showed fully matched that of the Europeans. They were the "dark companions," to borrow the title of a book by historian Donald Simpson. It was the Europeans who won all the acclaim, and the indispensable part played by rowers, porters, scouts, interpreters, and guides has too quickly been forgotten. Many of them were true professionals, compared to whom the Europeans often seem mere amateurs.

Some of the Africans took part in a sequence of expeditions, and in the space of a few years had covered far more miles than their employers. To have crossed Africa in the company of Stanley or Livingstone was an excellent reference, and entire careers were built upon the celebrity of these names. Not surprisingly, explorers were eager to take over the teams that had been employed by their predecessors and thus benefit from their experience.

These are the faithful followers of Speke and Grant. Livingstone paid tribute in his journal to the Africans who helped him to cross the continent with gifts of "10 slaughter oxen and 3 riding oxen," "large

who has accom

quantities of corn and earth nuts," "coarse beads and some hoes...much valued among the tribes to whom we are going. Everything that they could give...was freely bestowed.... I have reason to be thankful to Him who moved their hearts to liberality, and to them, to serve them in both temporal and spiritual things."

There were guides who as a result worked for four or five of the discoverers. Seedy Moobarik Bombay, a former slave of Yao descent, accompanied Burton in 1857, Speke in 1860, Stanley in 1871, and Cameron in 1876. Chuma, another freed Yao slave, traveled with Livingstone and on other expeditions, and the same was true of Susi.

The Royal Geographical Society was quick to recognize the achievement of these Africans, who were well known at that time for their good and faithful service. Eighteen men were awarded a medal after the Speke expedition, and sixty members of Livingstone's escort were decorated after his last journey. Some were even granted a small life pension; Bombay retired in comfort in 1876 after all his travels.

The Hazards of the Road

The Africans deserve all the more credit because employment on an expedition was no sinecure. Salaries were modest, ranging from $7 to $25 per year on Burton's expedition. (By contrast, Said bin Salim, his right-hand man, was paid $500.) More seriously, the workforce, however indispensable, was not always well

Chuma and Susi (above) accompanied Livingstone on his "voyages of discovery"— a misleading term, given the fact that the places discovered by Europeans were already known to the Africans.

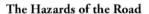

"Moobarik Bombay" ed Capt Speke during 2 Expeditions in Central Africa.

treated. Stanley was particularly known for his brutal methods.

The mortality rate among the Africans was horrendous. It rose from a low of some 20 percent to as much as 50 percent in the rainy season. The causes of death were many: fights, murder, drowning, fever (malaria and typhoid), dysentery, scurvy, attack by wild animals, overwork, and even starvation. The Europeans were not

The Africans, and sometimes the Arabs, had a good knowledge of the continent's geography. But it was not in their interest to spread information liable to attract covetous foreigners. Moobarik Bombay (left) went on Speke and Burton's expedition.

spared: All of Stanley's compatriots died in the course of his expedition to the Congo. The main cause of death in their case was disease.

Hunger and sickness were the common lot, and the explorers were haunted by fears of running short of food and drinking water. They were able to hunt and fish along the way, and where they could they bought food from the native population as they advanced.

Given the conditions, the large-scale desertions are hardly surprising. Of the ninety-eight men originally hired for Burton's expedition, fifty-five ran away during the journey. This meant there had to be more recruited at various stages, producing a mixture of different ethnic groups in the workforce.

Progress was often slow. Fifteen miles a day was reckoned a reasonable average, but there were occasions when it took several days to achieve that distance.

Among the difficulties that could beset an expedition there was the danger of attack by wild animals. But contrary to what one might imagine, mosquitoes were actually a much more fearsome enemy than crocodiles or

The tsetse fly (above) carries sleeping sickness, which affects humans and certain types of animals. The insect is unevenly distributed over the continent. When crossing the regions where this fly was rampant, Livingstone preferred to travel by night.

lions. Kingsley, who had a great aversion to mosquitoes, explained at length the best way of squashing a persistent insect: Rather than slapping it violently, approach it slowly with one's finger, then press down hard. She similarly described how, after traveling through a marsh, she had to rid herself of leeches clinging to her neck.

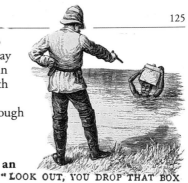

The Dissemination of Knowledge—and an Ideology to Go With It

"LOOK OUT, YOU DROP THAT BOX I'LL SHOOT YOU."

Explorers returning to Europe were often preceded by their reputation. Invited to give talks all over the country, they recounted their latest adventures to learned societies and women's groups.

Virtually all African explorers published book-length accounts of their travels, with the exception of Savorgnan de Brazza, who confined himself to writing only a few articles. Some bequeathed objects that they had acquired on their travels to scientific institutions. Kingsley's hat, for example, can now be admired

Stanley, here aiming at a porter, did not hesitate to use force, but serious cases were judged by representative tribunals set up on route. Five men were sentenced to death in this way, though three of them, two murderers and a deserter, were not executed.

at the Royal Geographical Society in London.

In the process of building up their reputations—which could bring them significant financial benefits—the explorers were informing the educated public about a little-known world. This was the great age of armchair travelers, whose journeys took place between the covers of their books.

These travel books call for comment: While they are among the rare sources of information on Africa, their contents are far from neutral and objective. They are colored by the ideology of the age, which was founded on a fundamental and constant belief in the superiority of the white man.

The Africans are thus always viewed through a distorting lens, and the authors tend, more or less consciously, to give the impression that they have been dealing with savages. Depicted as lazy, cowardly, lying, cruel, even degenerate, the Africans were presented as the personification of an astonishing accumulation of vices. The civilized society of western Europe is placed in opposition to the anarchy and license supposedly reigning in the tropics. Naturally, the travelers allowed for some exceptions, but they seemed the first to be surprised by them. It is worth noting, however, that some authors were less inclined than others to look down on African society. Livingstone and Kingsley were less blinkered by their preconceptions than Baker, for example.

The Limitations of Travel Literature

The explorers were at all events obliged to satisfy the expectations of a public that would have been disappointed not to shiver in horror at descriptions of cannibal feasts or wax indignant at reported scenes of debauchery. Thus one always finds a requisite passage on sensational subjects, rendered with humor by Kingsley and with sorrow or horror by other writers.

French officers stressed the depraved character of the Africans: "It was a strange feast. The men were shut in the huts while the women threw themselves into an orgy of frenzied dancing. From the oldest female to the children, all vied with each other in riotous noise and obscenity."

This portrait (left) is of Makoko, a Congo native leader.

The relative uniformity of travel writing was due also to the writers' widespread familiarity with the work of their predecessors. Without exactly plagiarizing, they were all strongly influenced by each other. There took place what one could call an internal exchange of information, which was often secondhand, if not even further removed from the source.

The explorers were in a privileged position as authors. Because they were writing "real life" stories, their readers never doubted the veracity of their books. For all their knowledge and their unquestionable geographical discoveries, these travelers presented to the public an image of Africa that was in many senses an imaginative reconstruction. Perhaps they could not have done otherwise. Are things any different today?

Travel books awakened an interest in Africa among the European and American upper classes, who were soon enjoying cruises down the Nile (below). Africa, a land of dreams made more accessible by the development of transport and the establishment of the colonial powers, also proved attractive to big-game hunters, who went on safari in the east and south of the continent.

DOCUMENTS

Explorers, patrons,
journalists, historians,
film directors, and novelists
present different perspectives
on a meeting of two worlds.

Preparing an Expedition

An expedition to Africa required expert organization and knowledge of the terrain. Explorers spent months drawing up their plans. Mary Kingsley started by looking in books and asking her friends. Sir Richard Burton, who had previous experience in Arabia, took particular care with his caravan.

The Call of the Tropics

It was in 1893 that, for the first time in my life, I found myself in possession of five or six months which were not heavily forestalled, and feeling like a boy with a new half-crown, I lay about in my mind, as Mr. Bunyan would say, as to what to do with them. "Go and learn your tropics," said Science. Where on earth am I to go, I wondered, for tropics are tropics wherever found, so I got down an atlas and saw that either South America or West Africa must be my destination, for the Malayan region was too far off and too expensive. Then I got Wallace's *Geographical Distribution* and after reading that master's article on the Ethiopian region I hardened my heart and closed with West Africa....

My ignorance regarding West Africa was soon removed. And although the vast cavity in my mind that it occupied is not even yet half filled up, there is a great deal of very curious information in its place. I use the word curious advisedly, for I think many seemed to

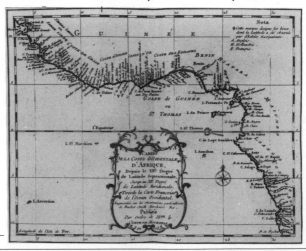

A 1739 French map of the coast of West Africa.

The British consulate in Zanzibar was a mandatory port of call for explorers in East Africa.

translate my request for practical hints and advice into an advertisement that "Rubbish may be shot here." This same information is in a state of great confusion still, although I have made heroic efforts to codify it....

I inquired of all my friends as a beginning what they knew of West Africa. The majority knew nothing. A percentage said, "Oh, you can't go there; that's where Sierra Leone is, the white man's grave, you know."...

No; there was no doubt about it, the place was not healthy.... So I next turned my attention to cross-examining the doctors. "Deadliest spot on earth," they said cheerfully, and showed me maps of the geographical distribution of disease. Now I do not say that a country looks inviting when it is coloured in Scheele's green or a bilious yellow, but these colours may arise from lack of artistic gift in the cartographer. There is no mistaking what he means by black, however, and black you'll find they colour West Africa from above Sierra Leone to below the Congo. "I wouldn't go there if I were you," said my medical friends, "you'll catch something."...

Naturally, while my higher intelligence was taken up with attending to these statements, my mind got set on going, and I had to go. Fortunately I could number among my acquaintances one individual who had lived on the Coast for seven years. Not, it is true, on that part of it which I was bound for. Still his advice was preeminently worth attention, because, in spite of his long residence in the deadliest spot of the region, he was still in fair going order. I told him I intended going to West Africa, and he said, "When you have made up your mind to go to West Africa the very best thing you can do is to get it unmade again and go to Scotland instead; but if your intelligence is not strong enough to do so, abstain from exposing yourself to the direct rays of the sun, take four grains of quinine every day for a fortnight before you reach the Rivers, and get some introductions to the Wesleyans; they are the only people on the Coast who have got a hearse with feathers."...

It was the beginning of August '93 when I first left England for "the Coast." Preparations of quinine with postage partially paid arrived up to the last moment, and a friend hastily sent two newspaper clippings, one entitled "A Week in a Palm-Oil Tub," which was supposed to describe the sort of accommodation, companions, and fauna likely to be met with on a steamer going to West Africa, and on which I was to spend seven to *The Graphic* contributor's one; the other from *The Daily Telegraph*, reviewing a French book of "Phrases in common use" in Dahomey. The opening sentence in the latter was, "Help, I am drowning." Then came the

inquiry, "If a man is not a thief?" and then another cry, "The boat is upset." "Get up, you lazy scamps," is the next exclamation, followed almost immediately by the question, "Why has this man not been buried?" "It is fetish that has killed him, and he must lie here exposed with nothing on him until only the bones remain," is the cheerful answer. This sounded discouraging to a person whose occupation would necessitate going about considerably in boats, and whose fixed desire was to study fetish. So with a feeling of foreboding gloom I left London for Liverpool—none the more cheerful for the matter-of-fact manner in which the steamboat agents had informed me that they did not issue return tickets by the West African lines of steamers.

Mary Kingsley
Travels in West Africa, 1897

The Composition of the Caravan

Before marching from Zungomero into the mountains I will order, for the reader's inspection, a muster of the party, and enlist his sympathies on

behalf of the unhappy being who had to lead it....

My companion's gun carrier, Seedy Mubarak [Moobarik] Bombay, a negro from Uhiao.... My henchman, Muinyi Mabruki, had been selected by his fellow-tribesman Bombay at Zanzibar; he was the slave of an Arab Shaykh, who willingly let him for the sum of five dollars per mensem. Mabruki is the type of bull-headed negro, low-browed, pig-eyed, pug-nosed, and provided by nature with that breadth and power, that massiveness and muscularity of jaw, which characterize the most voracious carnivores. He is at once the ugliest and the vainest of the party: His attention to his toilette knows no limit. His temper is execrable, ever in extremes, now wild with spirits, then dogged, depressed and surly, then fierce

and violent.... Bombay...became once more, what he before had been, a rara avis in the lands, an active servant and an honest man.

The Baloch are now to appear. My little party were servants of His Highness the Sayyid Majid of Zanzibar, who had detached them as an escort.... These men were armed with the usual matchlock [musket], the Cutch sabre, —one or two had Damascus blades,— the Indian hide-targe [shield], decorated with its usual tinsel, the long khanjar or dagger, extra matches, flints and steels, and toshdan, or ammunition pouches, sensibly distributed about their persons....

A proper regard to precedence induces me now to marshal the "sons of Ramji," who acted as interpreters, guides, and war-men. They were armed with the old "Tower-musket,"

Africans selling gold for liquor and guns, 19th century.

which, loaded with nearly an ounce of powder, they never allowed to quit the hand; and with those antiquated German-cavalry sabres which find their way all over the East.... They learned their power—without them I must have returned to the coast—and they presumed upon it...they swore not to carry burdens; they objected to loading and leading the asses; they would not bring up articles left behind in the camp or on the road; they claimed the sole right of buying provisions; they arrogated to themselves supreme command over the porters; and they pilfered from the loads whenever they wanted the luxuries of meat and beer; they drank deep; and on more than one occasion they endangered the caravan by their cavalier proceedings with the fair sex.... They had one short reply to all objections: the threat of desertion.

The donkey-men, five in number... were a trifle less manageable.... Lowest in rank, and little above the asses even in their own estimation, are the thirty-six Wanyamwezi Pagazi, or porters, who form the transport-corps....

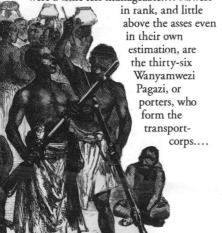

In portioning the loads there is always much trouble: Each individual has his favourite fancy.... They hate the inconvenience of boxes, unless light enough to be carried at both ends of a "Banghi"-pole by one man, or heavy enough to be slung between porters.

Moving Camp

About such time, 5 AM, the camp is fairly roused, and a little low chatting becomes audible. This is a critical moment. The porters have promised overnight, to start early, and to make a long wholesome march. But, "uncertain, coy, and hard to please," they change their minds like the fair sex, the cold morning makes them unlike the men of the warm evening, and perhaps one of them has fever. Moreover, in every caravan there is some lazy, loud-lunged, contradictory, and unmanageable fellow, whose sole delight is to give trouble. If no march be in prospect, they sit obstinately before the fire warming their hands and feet, inhaling the smoke with averted heads, and casting quizzical looks at their fuming and fidgety employer. If all be unanimous, it is vain to attempt them, even soft sawder is but "throwing comfits to cows." We return to our tent. If, however, there be a division, a little active stimulating will cause a march. Then a louder conversation leads to cries of Kwecha! Kwecha! Pakia! Pakia! Hopa! Hopa! Collect! pack! set out! Safari! Safari leo! a journey, a journey today! and some peculiarly African boasts, P'hunda! Ngami! I am an ass! a camel! accompanied by a roar of bawling voices, drumming, whistling, piping, and the braying of Barghumi, or horns.... My companion and I, when well enough to ride, mount our asses, led by the gunbearers, who carry all necessaries for offence and defence; when unfit for exercise, we are borne in hammocks, slung to long poles, and carried by two men at a time....

When all is ready, the Kirangozi or Mnyamwezi guide rises and shoulders his load, which is ever one of the lightest. He deliberately raises his furled flag, a plain blood-red, the sign of a caravan from Zanzibar, much tattered by the thorns....

The Kirangozi is followed by an Indian file, those nearest to him, the grandees of the gang, are heavily laden with ivories: When the weight of the tusk is inordinate, it is tied to a pole and is carried palanquin-fashion by two men. A large cow-bell, whose music rarely ceases on the march, is attached to the point which is to the fore; to the bamboo behind is lashed the porter's private baggage.... The ivory-carriers are succeeded by the bearers of cloth and beads.... Behind the cloth bearers straggles a long line of porters and slaves, laden with the lighter stuff, rhinoceros-teeth, hides, salt-cones, tobacco, brass wire, iron hoes, boxes and bags, beds and tents, pots and water-gourds, mats and private stores. With the Pagazi...march the armed slaves, who are never seen to quit their muskets, the women, and the little toddling children, who rarely fail to carry something, be it only of a pound weight, and the asses neatly laden with saddle-bags of giraffe or buffalo-hide.

A "Mganga" almost universally accompanies the caravan, not disdaining to act as a common porter. The "parson" not only claims, in virtue of his sacred calling, the lightest load; he is also a stout, smooth, and sleek-headed man, because, as usual with his

Speke's camp in the valley of Uthungu.

class, he eats much and works little....

On the road it is considered prudent as well as pleasurable to be as loud as possible, in order to impress upon plunderers an exaggerated idea of the caravan's strength; for equally good reasons silence is recommended in the kraal....

About 8 AM, when the fiery sun has topped the trees and a pool of water, or a shady place appears, the planting of the red flag, the braying of a Barghumi, or koodoo's horn, which, heard at a distance in the deep forests, has something of the charm which endears

the "Cor de Chasse" to every woodman's ear, and sometimes a musket-shot or two, announces a short halt. The porters stack their loads, and lie or loiter about for a few minutes, chatting, drinking, and smoking tobacco and bhang, with the usual whooping, screaming cough....

If the stage be prolonged towards noon, the caravan lags, straggles, and suffers sorely.... The Arabs and the Baloch must often halt to rest. The slaves ensconce themselves in snug places; the porters, propping their burdens against trees, curl up, dog-like under the shade.... The more energetic at once apply themselves to "making all snug" for the long hot afternoon and the nipping night; some hew down young trees, others collect heaps of leafy boughs....

When lodgings in the kraal have been distributed, and the animals have been off-packed, and water has been brought from the pit or stream, all apply themselves to the pleasant toil of refection. Merrily then sounds the breathless chant of the woman pounding or rubbing down grain, the song of the cook, and the tinkle-tinkle of the slave's pestle, as he bends over the iron mortar from which he stealthily abstracts the coffee.

Richard Burton
The Lake Regions of Central Africa
1860

The Explorers Confront Africa

Africa held plenty of surprises for the explorers, and the local customs, the splendors of the royal courts, the fauna and the flora were described many times over. A wide range of reactions—amused, admiring, astonished, compassionate, or arrogant— was provoked by the encounter with a new world.

Meeting the Emperor of Buganda

He [Mutesa] first took a deliberate survey of me, which I returned with interest, for he was as interesting to me as I was to him. His impression of me was that I was younger than Speke, not so tall, but better dressed....

I wrote that evening in my diary: "M[u]tesa has impressed me as being an intelligent and distinguished prince, who, if aided in time by virtuous philanthropists, will do more for Central Africa than fifty years of Gospel teaching, unaided by such authority, can do. I think I see in him...a prince well worthy of the most hearty sym-

pathies that Europe can give him."...

The chief reason for admiration lay, probably, in the surprise with which I viewed the man whom Speke had beheld as a boy—and who was described by him through about two hundred pages of his book as a vain, foolish, peevish, headstrong youth and a murderous despot—sedate and composed in manner, intelligent in his questions and remarks beyond anything I expected to meet in Africa. That I should see him so well-dressed, the centre of a court equally well-dressed and intelligent, that he should have

obtained supremacy over a great region into which moneyed strangers and soldiers from Cairo and Zanzibar flocked for...its supreme head, that his subjects should speak of him with respect, and his guests...honour him, were minor causes, which, I venture to consider, were sufficient to win my favourable judgment....

I am aware that there are negrophobists who may attribute this conduct of M[u]tesa to a natural gift for duplicity. He is undoubtedly a man who possesses great natural talents, but he also shows sometimes the waywardness, petulance, and withal the frank, exuberant, joyous moods, of youth. I will also admit that M[u]tesa can be *politic*...but he has also a child's unstudied ease of manner. I soon saw that he was highly clever, and possessed of the abilities to govern, but his cleverness and ability lacked the mannerisms of a European's....

A description of M[u]tesa's person was written in my diary on the third evening of my visit to him, from which I quote: "In person M[u]tesa is tall, probably 6 feet 1 inch, and slender. He has very intelligent and agreeable features, reminding me of some of the faces of the great stone images at Thebes, and of the statues in the Museum at Cairo. He has the same fullness of lips, but their grossness is relieved by the general expression of amiability blended with dignity that pervades his face, and the large, lustrous, lambent eyes that lend it a strange beauty, and are typical of the race from which I believe him to have sprung. His colour is of a dark red

Stanley is given a ceremonial welcome at the court of King Mutesa.

brown, of a wonderfully smooth surface. When not engaged in council, he throws off unreservedly the bearing that characterizes him when on the throne, and gives free rein to his humour, indulging in hearty peals of laughter. He seems to be interested in the discussion of the manners and customs of European courts, and to be enamoured of hearing of the wonders of civilization. He is ambitious to imitate as much as lies in his power the ways of the white man.…

On this day I recorded an interesting event which occurred in the morning. M[u]tesa, about 7 AM, sallied out of his quarters, accompanied by a host of guards, pages, standard bearers, fifers, drummers, chiefs, native guests, claimants, etc., and about two hundred women of his household, and as he passed by my courtyard, he sent one of his pages to request my presence. While he passed on, I…made as presentable an appearance as my clothes-bag enabled me, and then, accompanied by two of my boat's crew as gunbearers, followed the court to the lake.

M[u]tesa was seated on an iron stool, the centre of a large group of admiring women, who, as soon as I appeared, focused about two hundred pairs of lustrous, humid eyes on my person, at which he laughed.

"You see, Stamlee," said he, "how my women look at you; they expected to see you accompanied by a woman of your own colour. I am not jealous though. Come and sit down."

Presently M[u]tesa whispered an order to a page, who sprang to obey, and responding to his summons, there darted into view from the bend in Murchison Bay…forty

Mutesa and his dignitaries.

Despite initial reticence, some explorers joined in African festivities. Here James Grant is shown dancing with Ukulima.

magnificent canoes, all painted an ochreous brown, which I perceived to be the universally favourite colour. *En passant*, I have wondered whether they admire this colour from an idea that it resembles the dark bronze of their own bodies. For pure Waganda are not black by any means. The women and chiefs of M[u]tesa, who may furnish the best specimens of Waganda, are nearly all of a bronze or a dark reddish brown, with peculiar smooth, soft skins, rendered still more tender and velvety to the touch by their habit of shampooing with butter.... The national dress—which depended from the right shoulders of the larger number of those not immediately connected with the court were of a light brown also. It struck me, when I saw the brown skins, brown robes, and brown canoes, that brown must be the national colour.

Henry Morton Stanley
Through the Dark Continent, 1878

Burton and the Wanyamwezi

The Wanyamwezi tribe, the proprietors of the soil, is the typical race in this portion of Central Africa: Its comparative industry and commercial activity have secured to it a superiority over the other kindred races.

The aspect of the Wanyamwezi is alone sufficient to disprove the existence of very elevated lands in this part of the African interior. They are usually of a dark sepia-brown, rarely coloured like diluted Indian ink, as are the Wahiao and slave races to the south, with negroid features markedly less Semitic than the people of the eastern coast. The effluvium from their skins, especially after exercise or excitement, marks their connection with the negro. The hair curls crisply, but it grows to the length of four or five inches before it splits; it is usually twisted into many little ringlets or hanks; it hangs down like a fringe to the neck, and is combed off the forehead after the manner of the ancient Egyptians and the modern Hottentots. The beard is thin and short, there are no whiskers, and the moustachio—when not plucked out—is scant and straggling. Most of the men and nearly all the women remove the eyelashes, and pilar hair rarely appears to grow.

The normal figure of the race is tall and stout, and the women are remarkable for the elongation of the mammary organs. Few have small waists, and the only lean men in the land are the youths, the sick, and the famished. This race is said to be long-lived, and it is not deficient in bodily strength and savage courage.

The clan-mark is a double line of little cuts, like the marks of cupping, made by a friend with a knife or razor, along the temporal fossae from the external edges of the eyebrows to the middle of the cheeks or to the lower jaws. Sometimes a third line, or a band of three small lines, is drawn down the forehead to the bridge of the nose. The men prefer a black, charcoal being the substance generally used, the women a blue colour, and the latter sometimes ornament their faces with little perpendicular scars below the eyes. They do not file the teeth into a saw-shape as seen amongst the southern races, but they generally form an inner triangular or wedge-shaped aperture by chipping away the internal corners of the two front incisors like the Damaras, and the women extract the lower central teeth. Both sexes enlarge the [ear] lobes....

Another peculiarity of the Wanyamwezi is the position of the Wahárá, or unmarried girls. Until puberty they live in the father's house;

after that period the spinsters of the village, who usually number from seven to a dozen, assemble together and build for themselves at a distance from their homes a hut where they can receive their friends without parental interference. There is but one limit to community in single life: If the Mhárá, or "maiden," be likely to become a mother, her "young man" must marry her under pain of mulct; and if she die in childbirth, her father demands from her lover a large fine for having taken away his daughter's life. Marriage takes place when the youth can afford to pay the price for a wife: It varies according to circumstances from one to ten cows. The wife is so far the property of the husband that he can claim damages from the adulterer; he may not, however, sell her, except when in difficulties. The marriage is celebrated with the usual carouse, and the bridegroom takes up his quarters in his wife's home, not under her father's roof. Polygamy is the rule with the wealthy. There is little community of interests

The fauna of the Nile, as depicted in the late 17th century.

and apparently a lack of family affection in these tribes. The husband, when returning from the coast laden with cloth, will refuse a single shukkah to his wife, and the wife succeeding to an inheritance will abandon her husband to starvation. The man takes charge of the cattle, goats, sheep, and poultry; the woman has power over the grain and vegetables; and each must grow tobacco, having little hope of borrowing from the other.

Richard Burton,
*The Lake Regions
of Central Africa,* 1860

Kingsley Encounters a Crocodile

Now a crocodile drifting down in deep water, or lying asleep with its jaws open on a sand-bank in the sun, is a picturesque adornment to the landscape when you are on the deck of a steamer, and you can write

home about it and frighten your relations on your behalf; but when you are away among the swamps in a small dug-out canoe, and that crocodile and his relations are awake—a thing he

Livingstone is given an elephant tusk as a sign of welcome in a village on Lake Tanganyika.

makes a point of being at flood tide because of fish coming along—and when he has got his foot upon his native heath—that is to say, his tail within holding reach of his native mud —he is highly interesting, and you may not be able to write home about him— and you get frightened on your own behalf. For crocodiles can, and often do, in such places, grab at people in small canoes. I have known of several natives losing their lives in this way; some native villages are approachable from the main river by a short cut, as it were, through the mangrove swamps, and the inhabitants of such villages will now and then go across this way with small canoes instead of by the constant channel to the village, which is almost always winding. In addition to this unpleasantness you are liable…to get tide-trapped away in the swamps…and you find you cannot get back to the main river. For you cannot get out and drag your canoe across the stretches of

mud that separate you from it, because the mud is of too unstable a nature and too deep, and sinking into it means staying in it, at any rate until some geologist of the remote future may come across you, in a fossilized state, when that mangrove swamp shall have become dry land. Of course if you really want a truly safe investment in Fame, and really care about Posterity, and Posterity's Science, you will jump over into the black batter-like, stinking slime, cheered by the thought of the terrific sensation you will produce 20,000 years hence, and the care you will be taken of then by your fellow-creatures in a museum. But if you are a mere ordinary person of a retiring nature, like me, you stop in your lagoon until the tide rises again; most of your attention is directed to dealing with an "at home" to crocodiles and mangrove flies, and with the fearful stench of the slime round you. What little time you have over you will employ in wondering why you came to West Africa, and why, after having reached this point of absurdity, you need have gone and painted the lily and adorned the rose, by being such a colossal ass as to come fooling about in mangrove swamps. Twice this chatty little incident, as Lady MacDonald would call it, has happened to me, but never again if I can help it. On one occasion, the last, a mighty Silurian, as *The Daily Telegraph* would call him, chose to get his front paws over the stern of my canoe, and endeavoured to improve our acquaintance. I had to retire to the bows, to keep the balance right, and fetch him a clip on the snout with a paddle, when he withdrew, and I paddled into the very middle of the lagoon, hoping the water there was too deep for him or any of his friends to repeat the performance. Presumably it was, for no one did it again. I should think that crocodile was eight feet long; but don't go and say I measured him, or that this is my outside measurement for crocodiles. I have measured them when they have been killed by other people, fifteen, eighteen, and twenty-one feet odd. This was only a pushing young creature who had not learnt manners.

Mary Kingsley
Travels in West Africa, 1897

One Is Always a Stranger to Someone

There must be something in the appearance of white men, frightfully repulsive to the unsophisticated natives of Africa; for, on entering villages previously unvisited by Europeans, if we met a child coming quietly and unsuspectingly towards us, the moment he raised his eyes, and saw the men…he would take to his heels in an agony of terror…. Alarmed by the child's wild outcries, the mother rushes out of her hut, but darts back again at the first glimpse of the same fearful apparition. Dogs turn tail, and scour off in dismay; and hens, abandoning their chicks, fly screaming to the tops of the houses. The so lately peaceful village becomes a scene of confusion and hubbub, until calmed by the laughing assurance of our men, that white people do not eat black folks; a joke having often-times greater influence in Africa than solemn assertions.

David Livingstone
The Zambezi and Its Tributaries
1865

Samuel Baker Compares Black Men to White Men

The black man is a curious anomaly, the good and bad points of human nature bursting forth without any arrangement, like the flowers and thorns of his own wilderness. A creature of impulse, seldom actuated by reflection, the black man astounds by his complete obtuseness, and as suddenly confounds

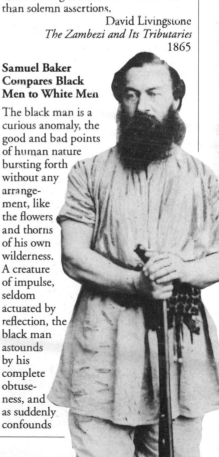

you by an unexpected exhibition of sympathy. From a long experience with African savages, I think it is as absurd to condemn the negro *in toto*, as it is preposterous to compare his intellectual capacity with that of the white man. It is unfortunately the fashion for one party to uphold the negro as a superior being, while the other denies him the common powers of reason.

So great a difference of opinion has ever existed upon the intrinsic value of the negro, that the very perplexity of the question is a proof that he is altogether a distinct variety. So long as it is generally considered that the negro and the white man are to be governed by the same laws and guided by the same management, so long will the former remain a thorn in the side of every community to which he may unhappily belong. When the horse and the ass shall be found to match in double harness, the white man and the black will pull together under the same régime. It is the grand error of equalizing that which is unequal, that has lowered the negro character, and made the black man a reproach.

In his savage home, what is the African? Certainly bad; but not so bad as white men would (I believe) be under similar circumstances. He is acted

upon by the bad passions inherent in human nature, but there is no exaggerated vice, such as is found in civilized countries. The strong takes from the weak, one tribe fights the other—do not perhaps we in Europe?—these are the legitimate acts of independent tribes, authorized by their chiefs. They mutually enslave each other—how long is it since America and *we ourselves* ceased to be slaveholders? He is callous and ungrateful—in Europe is there no ingratitude? He is cunning and a liar by nature—in Europe is all truth and sincerity?

Why should the black man not be equal to the white? He is as powerful in frame, why should he not be as exalted in mind? In childhood I believe the negro to be in advance, in intellectual quickness, of the white child of similar age, but the mind does not expand—it promises fruit, but does not ripen; and the negro man has grown in body, but not advanced in intellect....

Under peculiar guidance, and subject to a certain restraint, the negro may be an important and most useful being; but if treated as an Englishman, he will affect the vices but none of the virtues —of civilization, and his natural good qualities will be lost in his attempts to become a "white man."

Samuel Baker,
from *East African Explorers*, by James Place and Charles Richards, 1960

Livingstone in the Role of Savior

After resting a little, Mbame told us that a slave party on its way to Tete would presently pass through his village.

"Shall we interfere?" we inquired of each other. We remembered that all our valuable private baggage was in Tete, which, if we freed the slaves, might, together with some Government property, be destroyed in retaliation; but this system of slave-hunters dogging us where previously they durst not venture, and, on pretence of being "our children," setting one tribe against another, to furnish themselves with slaves, would so inevitably thwart all the efforts, for which we had the sanction of the Portuguese Government, that we resolved to run all risks, and put a stop, if possible, to the slave-trade, which had now followed on the footsteps of our discoveries.

Baker, always imperturbable, sizing up African warriors from his mount.

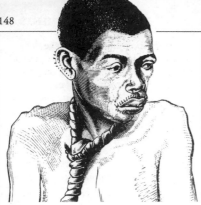

Engraving of a slave made in 1840.

A few minutes after Mbame had spoken to us, the slave party, a long line of manacled men, women, and children, came wending their way round the hill and into the valley, on the side of which the village stood.

The black drivers, armed with muskets, and bedecked with various articles of finery, marched jauntily in the front, middle, and rear of the line; some of them blowing exultant notes out of long tin horns. They seemed to feel that they were doing a very noble thing, and might proudly march with an air of triumph.

But the instant the fellows caught a glimpse of the English, they darted off like mad into the forest; so fast, indeed, that we caught but a glimpse of their red caps and the soles of their feet. The chief of the party alone remained; and he, from being in front, had his hand tightly grasped by a Makololo! He proved to be a well-known slave of the late Commandant at Tete, and for some time our own attendant while there.

On asking him how he obtained these captives, he replied, he had bought them; but on our inquiring of the people themselves all, save four, said they had been captured in war. While this inquiry was going on, he bolted too.

The captives knelt down, and, in their way of expressing thanks, clapped their hands with great energy. They were thus left entirely on our hands, and knives were soon busy at work cutting the women and children loose. It was more difficult to cut the men adrift, as each had his neck in the fork of a stout stick, six or seven feet long, and kept in by an iron rod which was riveted at both ends across the throat. With a saw, luckily in the Bishop's baggage, one by one the men were sawn out into freedom.

The women, on being told to take the meal they were carrying and cook breakfast for themselves and the children, seemed to consider the news too good to be true; but after a little coaxing went at it with alacrity, and made a capital fire by which to boil their pots with the slave sticks and bonds, their old acquaintance through many a sad night and weary day.

Many were mere children about five years of age and under. One little boy, with the simplicity of childhood, said to our men, "The others tied and starved us, you cut the ropes and tell us to eat; what sort of people are you? Where did you come from?"

Two of the women had been shot the day before for attempting to untie the thongs. This, the rest were told, was to prevent them from attempting to escape. One woman had her infant's brains knocked out, because she could not carry her load and it. And a man was despatched with an axe, because he had broken down with fatigue. Self-interest would have set a watch over the whole rather than commit murder; but in this traffic we invariably find self-interest overcome by contempt of human life and by bloodthirstiness.

David Livingstone
The Zambezi and Its Tributaries
1865

Although they condemned the slave trade, the explorers were often obliged to travel with slave caravans for their own safety.

The Advent of Colonialism

Even if they did not explicitly support colonialism, the explorers, by calling attention to the resources of the "Dark Continent," encouraged the European powers to establish a presence there. Some pioneers, it is true, had purely commercial ambitions, presenting no challenge to the authority of the African leaders; but from 1870 to 1880 the colonial cause had everyone in thrall.

Brazza's Treaties with Makoko

During the visit paid to me by the chiefs, while I was with Makoko, I explained to them that the white men's purpose in founding villages was to keep open the routes along which merchandise would come to their countries. And the villages needed to be situated on the riverbanks because the white men would arrive in canoes driven by fire. Not wanting to deprive myself of my merchandise, it was with some apprehension that I saw the time of my departure arrive. I made Makoko a present of eighteen lengths of good

Portrait of Pierre Savorgnan de Brazza, 1902.

A flag symbolized not so much a special alliance as the taking possession of territory.

cloth, mirrors, and a necklace, while expressing regret that I was unable, given the length of the route I had yet to cover, to make him a more substantial present. Makoko seemed pleased and gave me, on his side, fifty lengths of European cloth and three hundred pieces of local cloth. Then, on the day of my departure, he assembled all the neighboring chiefs (it was 10 September), took my hand in their presence and, placing it in that of Nganscumo, said: "I entrust to you this white man who has come to see us; if, when he has finished what he has to do, he wants to go to Nkouna, along the

river, you will take him there. If he wants to go overland, you will bring him here." Then, turning towards me, he said: "You have come here bearing us friendly words, you have lived among us and you have made us forget all we have heard about the white men; those who come after you will also be welcome and will be able to settle in this country if they wish it."...

A few days later twelve Obanghi chiefs, who had come to see me to arrange a peace treaty, made a large hole in the ground, into which the two most important chiefs threw a powder charge, a gun flint and some bullets; for

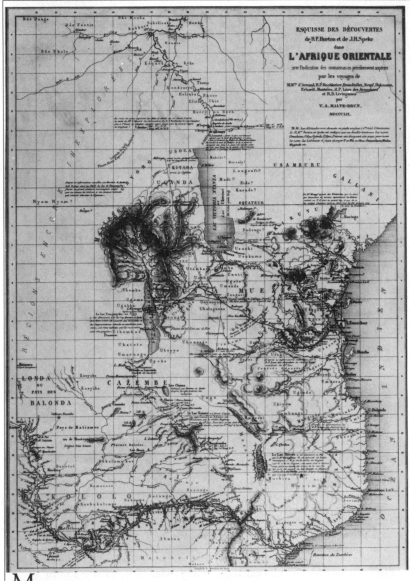

Map showing the new discoveries of Burton and Speke in 1859.

my part, I threw cartridges into the hole, then the hole was filled in, and so peace was agreed. After the bloody events to which the Congo and the Alima bore witness, during Stanley's voyage and my own, the first task to be carried out by the Europeans was that of appeasement and peace making. I am happy to have undertaken it and brought it to a successful conclusion.

My negotiations with the Abanko having been so satisfactorily concluded, it was decided that on my visit to Nkouna I would be accompanied by an Abanko chief, through whom I could bring the other chiefs, who were in Nkouna on business, up to date with the situation. On the first of October I arrived in Nkouna, where, in the presence of all the gathered chiefs, and on the strength of the powers vested in me by Makoko, I took possession of the second French base in West Africa.

Savorgnan de Brazza
quoted in Henri Brunschwig
Brazza l'Explorateur, 1972

Cameron's Optimism

The whole trade of tropical Africa is at present dependent on human beings as beasts of burden, and valuable labour which might be profitably employed in cultivating the ground or collecting products for exportation is thus lost....

Ivory is not likely to last for ever (or for long) as the main export from Africa; indeed the ruthless manner in which the elephants are destroyed and harassed has already begun to show its effects. In places where elephants were by no means uncommon a few years ago, their wanton destruction has had its natural effect, and they are now rarely encountered.

Having this probable extinction of

Portrait of Verney Lovett Cameron, 1877.

the ivory trade in view, and allowing, as all sensible people must, that legitimate commerce is the proper way to open up and civilize a country, we must see what other lucrative sources of trade may hereafter replace that in ivory.

Fortunately we have not far to go; for the vegetable and mineral products of this marvellous land are equal in value, variety, and quantity to those of the most favoured portions of the globe. And if the inhabitants can be employed in their exploitation, vast fortunes will reward those who may be the pioneers of commerce; but the first step necessary towards this is the establishment of proper means of communication....

Missionary efforts will not avail to stop the slave-trade and open the country to civilization unless supplemented by commerce. Commercial enterprise and missionary effort, instead of acting in opposition, as is too often the case, should do their best to assist each other. Wherever commerce finds its way, there missionaries will follow; and wherever missionaries prove that white men can live and travel, there trade is certain to be established....

I would recommend the acquirement of a port—Mombasa for instance—from the Sultan of Zanzibar, by treaty or purchase, and thence to run a light line of railway to the Tanganyika, via Unyanyembe, with branches to the Victoria Nyanza, and to the southward through Ugogo…. Such a railway advancing into the country would at once begin to make a return, for the present ivory trade to Zanzibar should be sufficient to pay working expenses and leave a margin for profit, without making any allowance for the increased trade….

Many people may say that the rights of native chiefs to govern their countries must not be interfered with. I doubt whether there is a country in Central Africa where the people would not soon welcome and rally round a settled form of government. The rule of the chiefs over their subjects is capricious and barbarous, and death or mutilation is ordered and carried out at the nod of a drunken despot….

I firmly believe that opening up proper lines of communication will do much to check the cursed traffic in human flesh, and that the extension of legitimate commerce will ultimately put an end to it altogether.

Verney Lovett Cameron
Across Africa, 1877

Livingstone's Mission

The races of this Continent seem to have advanced to a certain point and no further; their progress in the arts of working iron and copper, in pottery, basket-making, spinning, weaving, making nets, fish-hooks, spears, axes, knives, needles, and other things, whether originally invented by this people or communicated by another instructor, appears to have remained in the same rude state for a great number of centuries. This apparent stagnation of mind in certain nations we cannot understand; but, since we have in the later ages of the world made what we consider great progress in the arts, we have unconsciously got into the way of speaking of some other races in much the same tone as that used by the Celestials in the Flowery Land. These same Chinese anticipated us in several most important discoveries by as many centuries as we may have preceded others. In the knowledge of the properties of the magnet, the composition of gunpowder,

The rivers of Africa disappointed hopeful explorers, for steamboats were unable to navigate the rapids.

the invention of printing, the manufacture of porcelain, of silk, and in the progress of literature, they were before us. But then the power of making further discoveries was arrested, and a stagnation of the intellect prevented their advancing in the path of improvement or invention. To the Asiatics we owe cotton, sugar, clepsydras, and sundials. From the East we have derived algebra, the game of chess, coffee, tea, alcohol, and steel. The servile imitation, which took the place of mental activity and invention, seems to have fallen on Chinese, Japanese, Asiatics, Arabians, and Africans alike. Does this paralysis of the inventive faculties indicate that each race is destined to perform its own part in the one vast plan of creative Providence, of which our finite minds can take in only so minute a portion that we shall never comprehend it as a whole till the end of all things?…

I propose to go inland…and endeavour to commence that system on the East which has been so eminently successful on the West Coast; a system combining the repressive efforts of H.M. cruisers with lawful trade and Christian Missions—the moral and material results of which have been so gratifying. I hope to ascend the Ruvuma,…and…shall strive, by passing along the Northern end of Lake Nyasa and round the Southern end of Lake Tanganyika, to ascertain the watershed of that part of Africa. In so doing, I have no wish to unsettle what with so much toil and danger was accomplished by Speke and Grant, but rather to confirm their illustrious discoveries.

David Livingstone
The Zambezi and Its Tributaries
1865

The Explorer's Changing Image

Two admiring novelists, Livingstone's eulogizer, and a contemporary African historian all present different points of view about great explorers.

A Slave Party Set Free

"Who are you?" she said. "The other people tied and starved us, but you cut the ropes and tell us to eat; what sort of people are you? Where did you come from?"

To this Harold replied briefly that he was an Englishman, who hated slavers and slavery, but he said nothing more at that time, as he intended to have a palaver and explanation with the freed captives after their meal was over.

There was a great clapping of hands among the slaves, expressive of gratitude, on hearing that they were free....

When the oldest man of the party, who appeared to be between twenty and thirty, was brought forward and questioned, he gave some interesting and startling information.

"Tell him," said Harold, "that we are Englishmen; that we belong to the same nation as the great white man Dr. Livingstone, who travelled through this land some years ago—the nation which hates slavery because the Great God hates it, and would have all men to be free, to serve each other in love, and to do to other people as they would have other people do to them. Ask him also where he comes from, and who captured him and his companions."

To this the negro replied—"What the white man says may be true, but the white men seem to tell lies too much. The men who killed our

R ight: Burton and Speke, as depicted in *Mountains of the Moon*, 1990, the film of William Harrison's 1982 book.

warriors, burned our villages, and took our women and children away, came to us saying that they were friends; that they were the servants of the same people as the white man Livingstone, and wanted to trade with us. When we believed and trusted them, and were off our guard, they fired on us with their guns. We know not what to think or to believe."

Harold was much perplexed by this reply, for he knew not what evidence to cite in proof that he, at least, was not a deceiver.

"Tell him," he said at length, "that there are false white men as well as true, and that the best proof I can give him that I am one of the true is, to set him and his friends at liberty. They are now as free to go where they please as we are."

Robert M. Ballantyne
Black Ivory, 1873

Burton and Speke Through the Eyes of a Novelist

"I found the lake," he said, at last. "And I'm completely convinced that it's the principal feeder of the Nile. In a way, I know this is just assertion without proof, but I did take a number of thermometer readings, and I know I'm right. I also want to make clear that this is my discovery."

Burton sat silent, not knowing what to say. The implication that what had happened was not a victory for the expedition, but only a personal one for Speke, took him by surprise.

"Well, I'm happy, Jack, that you've had a personal success," he managed.

"The thermometer readings put the altitude of the lake at about thirty-six hundred feet," Speke said. "I know I'm right. This is the main source of the Nile."

"What evidence do you have apart from thermometer readings?"

"The word of Arabs who have lived around the lake all their lives. I place the upper reaches of the lake at, oh, four or five degrees latitude."

Burton ate a fig, then drank some tea.

"Twenty years ago, my dear Jack," he said finally, "an Egyptian expedition sent by the late Mohammed Ali Pasha reached three degrees twenty-two minutes north latitude. If what you say is true, they would have sailed fifty miles out into the Nyanza. And the Egyptians never even heard of a lake, Jack! Never even *heard* of a lake!"

"Well, that's my information," Speke said.

Burton drank off his tea, watching his companion. Speke ate heartily.

"You don't speak Arabic," Burton went on. "How did you talk with these Arabs? Did you use Bombay as interpreter? You know that he has only a poor smattering of a single dialect of Arab himself. Are you sure that you didn't misunderstand?"

"I know I'm right about this! That's all I can say! I *know*...."

William Harrison
Burton and Speke, 1982

Livingstone Eulogized by Sir Bartle Frere

Undoubtedly his own great powers, natural and acquired, were one great element in his success. The qualifications necessary to constitute a complete traveller are so many and various, that they are seldom found in any one man; but Livingstone

L ivingstone, in a 1925 silent film called *Stanley and Livingstone*.

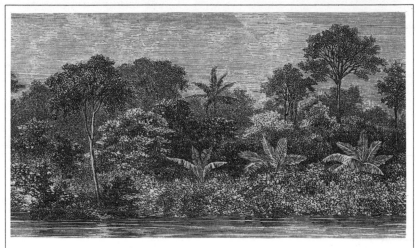

The banks of the Ogooué, 1876.

appeared to possess them all in a most exalted degree. His personal coolness and bravery, undisturbed and undaunted in any emergency, his wonderful tenacity of purpose, his gentleness and yet firmness in dealing with the native Africans, his self-negation and power of endurance, his iron frame and its capacity of resistance to all bad climatic influences, all these greatly contributed to success; whilst the wide and extended view he had of the duties of his sacred calling, gave to his character an elevation and power far beyond what the highest mental or physical gifts could have commanded....

As a whole, the work of his life will surely be held up in ages to come as one of singular nobleness of design, and of unflinching energy and self-sacrifice in execution. It will be long ere any one man will be able to open so large an extent of unknown land to civilized mankind. Yet longer, perhaps, ere we find a brighter example of a life of such continued and useful self-devotion to a noble cause.

> Sir Henry Bartle Frere,
> *Obituary of Livingstone: Address to the Royal Geographical Society*,
> 1874

An African Historian on Livingstone

For the Africans of the 19th century, Livingstone was but a transient European. The tribute that he paid to Africa may seem heavy: He lost a child and his wife, he himself died there. Nonetheless...Livingstone is not part of the history of Africa: He is part of the long history of colonization. On Africa he did no more than cast an eye, in a way that was undoubtedly lasting, and perspicacious, but also heavily colored by inherited ideas and ideological inventions.

> Elikia M'Bokolo, introduction to a French translation of Livingstone's *The Zambezi and its Tributaries*,
> 1981

Patrons

Governments and scientific societies were more than patrons: In addition to providing financial support, they initiated expeditions, followed their progress, and rewarded success. The explorers' celebrity depended upon these institutions.

Headquarters of the Royal Geographical Society (1854–70) at Whitehall Place in London.

Awarding the Patron's Gold Medal to Captain James A. Grant

In presenting the Patron's Medal to Captain Grant, Sir Roderick [Murchison] [said]:

"CAPTAIN GRANT, Eleven months have elapsed since we received your leader, Captain Speke, and yourself within these walls, with the cordial acknowledgment of the great services you had performed in opening out Eastern Equatorial Africa, and in showing how the White Nile flowed from the very lake previously discovered by your distinguished companion. Captain Speke having, on his arrival at Gondokoro, received the Medal most justly granted to him for the great discovery of Lake Victoria Nyanza, we, in conferring this Medal upon you, wish it to be understood that we once more emphatically mark our deep sense

of the value of the first great exploration of those lands around it, made by Captain Speke and yourself.

"When you returned here our Anniversary had passed over, and both our Medals had been adjudicated, or you would, doubtless, before now, have received the highest honour which we have it in our power to bestow. It was, however, a source of true gratification to us to see that the King of Italy was, in the mean time, foremost in recognizing your merit, as well as that of your skilful leader, and affixed to each of his Medals the appropriate motto of *Honor a Nilo!*

"On my own part I can truly say that, on the many occasions on which it has been my lot to present Medals to Explorers of distant regions, I never had greater satisfaction than on the present occasion. For now that I hand to you this Medal, bearing the effigy of Queen Victoria, I feel that we Geographers are not merely recompensing the noble and disinterested companion of Speke, but, as a soldier of the olden time myself, I have a special pride in recognizing in you the gallant young Officer, who, in the Indian mutiny, and despite a severe wound, was the means of saving from serious disaster the rear-guard of the illustrious Havelock, as he advanced to the relief of Lucknow.

"Accept, then, this, our gracious Patron's Medal, and consider it as our Victoria Cross."

Captain GRANT then replied: "Sir Roderick Murchison and Gentlemen —It was during a recent sojourn on the Continent that I received the communication from the Council of the Royal Geographical Society, announcing that they had unanimously awarded me one of their Gold Medals of the year. I assure you the receipt of this communi-

Speke and Grant in the field.

cation gave me intense pleasure; but it was a surprise to me, for I little thought I had done anything to merit so high and distinguished an honour. And to receive the Medal from your hands, Sir, from whom I have always experienced so much kindness, enhances the value of a gift which I shall cherish to my dying day. I feel so much embarrassed by the distinction you have conferred upon me, that I am quite unprepared to express myself in the language I should wish. I hope, therefore, you will excuse the few words in which I thank you for the honour you have done me."

Journal of the Royal Geographical Society, 1864

"Find Livingstone"

On the 16th October, in the year of our Lord 1869, I am in Madrid, fresh from the carnage at Valencia. At 10 AM Jacopo, at No.— Calle de la Cruz, hands me a telegram:…"Come to Paris on important business." The telegram is from Jas. Gordon Bennett, jun., the young manager of the New York *Herald*.…

At 3 PM I was on my way, and…did not arrive at Paris until the following night. I went straight to the "Grand Hotel," and knocked at the door of Mr. Bennett's room.

"Come in," I heard a voice say.

Entering, I found Mr. Bennett in bed.

"Who are you?" he asked.

"My name is Stanley!" I answered.

"Ah, yes! sit down; I have important business on hand for you."

After throwing over his shoulders his robe-de-chambre, Mr. Bennett asked, "Where do you think Livingstone is?"

"I really do not know, sir!"

"Do you think he is alive?"

"He may be, and he may not be!" I answered.

"Well, I think he is alive, and that he can be found, and I am going to send you to find him."

"What!" said I, "do you really think I can find Dr. Livingstone? Do you mean me to go to Central Africa?"

"Yes; I mean that you shall go, and find him wherever you may hear that he is, and to get what news you can of him, and perhaps"—delivering himself thoughtfully and deliberately—"the old man may be in want:—take enough with you to help him should he require it. Of course you will act according to your own plans, and do what you think best—BUT FIND LIVINGSTONE!"

Said I, wondering at the cool order of sending one to Central Africa to search for a man whom I, in common with almost all other men, believed to be dead, "have you considered seriously the great expense you are likely to incur on account of this little journey?"

"What will it cost?" he asked.…

"Burton and Speke's journey to Central Africa cost between £3000 and £5000, and I fear it cannot be done under £2500."

"Well, I will tell you what you will do. Draw a thousand pounds now; and when you have gone through that, draw another thousand, and when that is spent, draw another thousand, and when you have finished that, draw another thousand, and so on; but, FIND LIVINGSTONE."…

"Do you mean me to go straight on to Africa to search for Dr. Livingstone?"

"No! I wish you to go to the

James Gordon Bennett, manager of the New York *Herald*.

inauguration of the Suez Canal first and then proceed up the Nile. I hear Baker is about starting for Upper Egypt. Find out what you can about his expedition, and as you go up describe as well as possible whatever is interesting for tourists; and then write up a guide —a practical one for Lower Egypt, tell us about whatever is worth seeing and how to see it.... Then you might as well go to Jerusalem... Then visit Constantinople... From thence you may get through Persia to India.... Then...you can go after Livingstone. Probably you will hear by that time that Livingstone is on his way to Zanzibar; but if not, go into the interior and find him, if alive. Get what news of his discoveries you can; and, if you find he is dead, bring all possible proofs of his being dead. That is all. Good-night, and God be with you."

Henry Morton Stanley
How I Found Livingstone, 1872

The Burial of Livingstone

Livingstone's remains were buried in Westminster Abbey on 18 April 1874. The pall bearers were Sir Thomas Steele and W. F. Webb, old friends of the explorer, to whom he had given hospitality in the south of Africa where they had gone to hunt big game in the desert; Mr. Oswell, another great game-hunter, who discovered Lake Ngami with Livingstone; Doctor J. Kirk, a naturalist on the Zambezi expedition; the Reverend Horace Waller, a member of the Upper Shire mission; J. Young, leader of the first expedition sent in search of Livingstone; Henry Stanley, who found him at Ujiji; and Jacob Wainwright, representing the caravan. Livingstone's four children, his two sisters, his brother's wife, and the

Livingstone's funeral at Westminster Abbey.

Reverend Moffat, whose daughter he had married at Kuruman, followed the coffin. Behind them came the Duke of Sutherland, Lord Advocate of Scotland, Lord Houghton, Sir Bartle Frere, a long procession of celebrities, many representatives of the Geographical Society and the learned world of Great Britain.

The plaque over Livingstone's grave reads:

BROUGHT BY FAITHFUL HANDS
OVER LAND AND SEA
HERE RESTS
DAVID LIVINGSTONE,
MISSIONARY,
TRAVELLER,
PHILANTHROPIST,
BORN MARCH 19, 1813,
AT BLANTYRE, LANARKSHIRE,
DIED MAY 1 1873,
AT CHITAMBO VILLAGE, ULALA.

In December 1878, less than a year after his return, Stanley was sent back to the Congo by Belgium. His first task was to build a railway (below right) to Stanley Pool, bypassing the rapids.

Stanley and Leopold II

When I finally reached Europe in January 1878...little did I imagine that before the close of the year I should be preparing another expedition for the banks of that river on which we had suffered so greatly. But at Marseilles railway station, as I descended from the express just arrived from Italy, two Commissioners from His Majesty the King of the Belgians, Leopold II, met me, and before I was two hours older I was made aware that King Leopold intended to undertake to do something substantial for Africa, and that I was expected to assist him....

Any person acquainted with what I had so recently undergone can well imagine the reluctance with which I listened to the suggestion that I should return to the scene of so much disaster and suffering, though I heartily agreed...that it was a great and good work that the King was inclined to perform.... I was quite willing to give

my best advice, and to furnish those details necessary for the complete equipment of an expedition…but, "as for myself," I said, "I am so sick and weary that I cannot think with patience of any suggestion that I should personally conduct it."…

Early in November 1878 I received an invitation to be at the Royal Palace in Brussels at a certain date and hour. Punctual to the time, I there discovered various persons of more or less note in the commercial and monetary world… and presently we were all ushered into the council-room. After a few minutes it transpired that the object of the meeting was to consider the best way of promoting the very modest enterprise of studying what might be made of the Congo River and its basin. This body of gentlemen desired to know how much of the Congo River was actually navigable by light-draught vessels? What protection could friendly native chiefs give to commercial enterprises? Were the tribes along the Congo sufficiently intelligent to understand that it would be better for their interests to maintain a friendly intercourse with the whites than to restrict it? What tributes, taxes, or imports, if any, would be levied by the native chiefs for right of way through their country? What was the character of the produce which the natives would be able to exchange for European fabrics?… Some of the above questions were answerable even then, others were not. It was therefore resolved that a fund should be subscribed to equip an expedition to obtain accurate information; the subscribers to the fund assuming the name and title of "Comité d'Etudes du Haut Congo."

Henry Morton Stanley,
*The Congo and the Founding
of Its Free State*, 1885

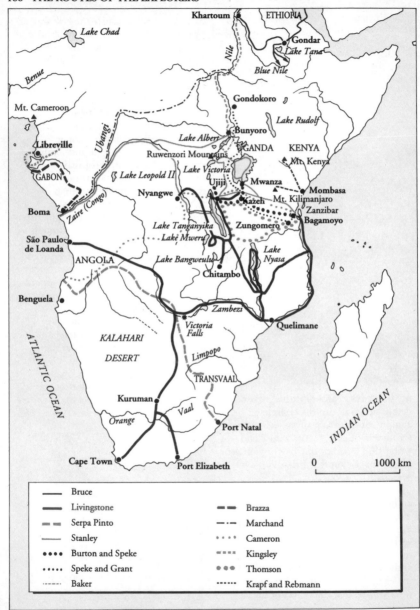

Chronology

1768–73
James Bruce travels in Abyssinia (Ethiopia) and to the sources of the Blue Nile
1788
The African Association founded in London by Sir Joseph Banks
1807–11
The British government abolishes the slave trade
1808
Slave trade prohibited in the United States after 1 January 1808
1815
The French government abolishes the slave trade
1820–2
Egyptian expedition to the confluence of the two Niles
1830
The Royal Geographical Society founded in London
1840
David Livingstone travels to South Africa
1840–53
Expeditions of missionaries Johann Ludwig Krapf and Johannes Rebmann
1848
Discovery of Mount Kilimanjaro (in Tanzania) by Johannes Rebmann
1849
Discovery of Mount Kenya (in Kenya) by Johann Ludwig Krapf
1849
Livingstone explores Lake Ngami (in northwest Botswana)
1853–4
Livingstone's expedition, helped by the Makololo, to the west coast of Africa
1855–6
Livingstone's expedition

to the east coast of Africa. Discovery of Victoria Falls in southern Africa
1856
Zanzibar declares independence from Oman. The rise of British influence
1856–7
Paul Du Chaillu travels to the Crystal Mountains in Central Africa
1857–8
Richard Burton and John Hanning Speke search for the sources of the Nile. Discovery of Lake Tanganyika and Victoria Nyanza in eastern Africa, between Zaire and Tanzania
1858–61
Livingstone's expedition on the Zambezi River. Discovery of Lake Nyasa in southeast Africa
1860–3
Speke and James Augustus Grant's expedition to Victoria Nyanza. They confirm that the White Nile has its source there
1863
Samuel and Florence Baker set off in search of Speke and Grant
1864
Death of Speke
1864
The Bakers reach Lake Albert, between Uganda and Zaire, the second source of the White Nile
1866–71
Livingstone's last series of expeditions south of the Great Lakes. He discovers Lake Mweru (between Zaire and Zambia) and Lake Bangweulu (in northern Zambia)

1869
Opening of the Suez Canal in Egypt
1871
Henry Morton Stanley sets off in search of Livingstone, and finds him at Ujiji on Lake Tanganyika
1873
The sultan of Zanzibar abolishes the slave trade under pressure from the British
May 1873
Livingstone dies in Africa
1873–5
Verney Lovett Cameron's expedition from Zanzibar to the west coast
1874–7
Stanley's expedition to Victoria Nyanza and Lake Tanganyika and down the Congo. Discovery of Lake Edward between Zaire and Uganda
April 1874
Livingstone's funeral in Westminster Abbey, London
1875–7
Pierre Savorgnan de Brazza's first expedition on the Ogooué and lower Congo rivers
1876
The Association Internationale Africaine founded by King Leopold II of Belgium
1879–84
Stanley works for Leopold II, colonizing and developing the Congo
1880–1
Brazza's second expedition. Franceville founded in southeast Gabon. Makoko accepts French protectorate status

1882
British occupation of Egypt
1883
Joseph Thomson travels from Mombasa, Kenya, to Lake Victoria across the Masai territories
1883–5
Third Brazza expedition. The occupation of the Congo begins. (Brazza appointed commissioner-general in 1886)
November 1884–February 1885
At the Berlin Conference on African Affairs the European powers debate the colonization of Africa, particularly the Congo
1885
The Congo becomes a Belgian protectorate under Leopold II and is known as the Congo Free State
1887–9
Stanley's last expedition, to free Emin Pasha
1890
British protectorate of Zanzibar
1893
Mary Kingsley's first expedition
1894
Uganda becomes British protectorate
1894–5
Kingsley's second expedition, crossing the regions between the Ogooué and Rembwe rivers
1898
Fashoda Incident: the climax of Franco-British rivalry in Africa
1912
Except for Egypt, Ethiopia, and Liberia, all of Africa is under European colonial rule

Further Reading

ON AFRICAN EXPLORERS AND EXPLORATION

Brodie, Fawn, *The Devil Drives: A Life of Sir Richard Burton*, Norton, New York, 1984

Burton, Isabel, *The Life of Captain Richard Burton*, Chapman and Hall, London, 1893

Forbath, Peter, *The River Congo*, Harper and Row, New York, 1977

Frank, Katherine, *A Voyager Out: The Life of Mary Kingsley*, Houghton Mifflin, Boston, 1986

Hall, Richard, *Stanley: An Adventurer Explored*, Collins, London, 1974

Hibbert, Christopher, *Africa Explored: Europeans in the Dark Continent, 1769–1889*, Allen Lane, London, 1982

Huxley, Elspeth, *Livingstone and His African Journeys*, Weidenfeld and Nicolson, London, 1974

Keay, John (general ed.), *The Royal Geographical Society History of World Exploration*, Hamlyn, London, 1991

Moorehead, Alan, *The Blue Nile*, Random House, New York, 1983

———, *The White Nile*, Hamish Hamilton, London, 1960

Place, James B., and Charles G. Richards, *East African Explorers*, Oxford University Press, London, 1960

Rotberg, Robert (ed.), *Africa and Its Explorers: Motives, Methods, and Impact*, Harvard University Press, Cambridge, Massachusetts, 1970

Severin, Timothy, *The African Adventure: A History of Africa's Explorers*, Hamish Hamilton, London, 1973

Simpson, Donald H., *Dark Companions: The African Contribution to the European Exploration of East Africa*, Elek, London, 1975

ON THE HISTORICAL AND CULTURAL BACKGROUND

Cairns, Hugh Alan, *Prelude to Imperialism: British Reactions to Central African Society 1840–90*, Routledge & Kegan Paul, London, 1965

Curtin, Philip, *The Image of Africa: British Ideas and Action 1780–1850*, University of Wisconsin Press, Madison, 1963

Kerchache, Jacques, *Art of Africa*, Harry N. Abrams, New York, 1993

Monti, Nicholas, *Africa Then: Photographs 1840–1918*, Thames and Hudson, London, 1987

Pakenham, Thomas, *The Scramble for Africa*, Weidenfeld and Nicolson, London, 1991

Sheriff, Abdul, *Slaves, Spices and Ivory in Zanzibar*, Ohio University Press, Athens, 1987

Willett, Frank, *African Art*, Thames and Hudson, London, 1986

WORKS BY THE EXPLORERS THEMSELVES

Baker, Samuel, *The Albert Nyanza*, Macmillan and Co., London, 1866

Bruce, James, *Travels to Discover the Source of the Nile in the Years 1768, 1769, 1770, 1771, 1772, and 1773*, 4 vols., Gregg International, Brookfield, Vermont, repr. of 1790 ed.

Burton, Richard F., *First Footsteps in East Africa: or an Exploration of Harar*, AMS Press, New York, repr. of 1856 ed.

———, *The Lake Regions of Central Africa*, Longman and Co., London, 1860

———, *Zanzibar: City, Island and Coast*, 2 vols, Tinsley Bros., London, 1872

Cameron, Verney Lovett, *Across Africa*, 2 vols., Johnson Reprint Corp., New York, repr. of 1877 ed.

Du Chaillu, Paul, *Explorations and Adventures in Equatorial Africa*, Johnson Reprint Corp., New York, repr. of 1871 ed.

———, *A Journey to Ashango-Land and Further Penetration into Equatorial Africa*, Johnson Reprint Corp., New York, repr. of 1867 ed.

Grant, James Augustus, *A Walk Across Africa*, AMS Press, New York, repr. of 1864 ed.

Kingsley, Mary, *Travels in West Africa*, Beacon Press, Boston, Massachusetts, 1988

———, *West African Studies*, Biblio Distribution Center, Lanham, Maryland, 1964

Krapf, Johann Ludwig, *Travels, Researches and Missionary Labours During an Eighteen Years' Residence in Eastern Africa*, Biblio Distribution Center, Lanham, Maryland, repr. of 1860 ed.

Livingstone, David, *The Last Journals of David Livingstone in Central Africa*, Greenwood Publishing Group, Westport, Connecticut, repr. of 1874 ed.

———, *Missionary Travels and Researches in South Africa*, Ayer Co. Pubs., Salem, New Hampshire, repr. of 1857 ed.

———, *Narrative of an Expedition to the Zambezi and Its Tributaries*, Johnson Reprint Corp., repr. of 1866 ed.

————, (ed. Isaac Schapera) *Private Journals, 1851–3*, Chatto & Windus, London, 1960; *Family Letters, 1841–56*, Chatto & Windus, London, 1961; *Missionary Correspondence, 1841–56*, Chatto & Windus, London, 1961

Speke, John Hanning, *Journal of the Discovery of the Source of the Nile*, 1863

Stanley, Henry Morton, *The Congo and the Founding of Its Free State*, 2 vols., Sampson Low & Co., London, 1885

————, (ed. Richard Stanley and Alan Neame) *The Exploration Diaries of Henry Morton Stanley*, William Kimber, London, 1961

————, *How I Found Livingstone*, Ayer Co.,

Pubs., Salem, New Hampshire, repr. of 1872 ed.

————, *In Darkest Africa*, Sampson Low & Co., London, 1890

————, *Through the Dark Continent*, 2 vols., Dover, New York, 1988

Thomson, Joseph, *To the Central African Lakes and Back*,

Biblio Distribution Center, Lanham, Maryland, repr. of 1881 ed.

————, *Through Masai Land: A Journey of Exploration among the Snowclad Volcanic Mountains and Strange Tribes of Eastern Equatorial Africa*, Sampson Low & Co., London, 1883

List of Illustrations

Index

Photograph Credits

All rights reserved 1, 2–3, 4–5, 6–7, 8–9, 10–1, 39, 55a, 56a, 56–7b, 57a, 62–3b, 68–9b, 73a, 74–5, 76b, 80c, 84b, 84–5a, 85, 86b, 90a, 93b, 124a, 124–5b, 132–3, 146–7, 155, 159, 163, front cover; T. and R. Annan, Glasgow 80b, 154; Bibliothèque Nationale, Paris 41, 42a, 42–3b, 45a, 46l, 53ar, 65a, 87b, 93a, 95c, 99b, 103, 106, 107a, 123a, 125a, 131, 136–7, 138–9, 141, 144, 152; Bridgeman archive 19a, 30a, 36b, 37, 38a, 38b, 40, 54a, 68a, 70, 72–3b, 76a, 77; British Film Institute, London 158; *Cahiers du Cinéma* 157; Jean-Loup Charmet 120–1, 128; Dagli-Orti 14, 17, 29b, 43a, 44a, 46r, 47b, 79, 88, 89, 102b, 104, 108, 119a, 126–7, 142–3, 161; Edimédia 18a, 20a, 22–3a, 28, 44b, 49, 51ar, 53b, 90a, 98, 99a, 140; Erica Graham OBE 62a, 96a, 112b; E.T. archive 78a, 80–1, 111a, 113b, 119b; Explorer archive 20b, 47a, 69c, 71, 82a, 82b, 117c, 130, 134, 148; Hoa-Qui 15, 29a, 35l, 105b, 107b; Mansell Collection 66, 86–7a; Musée Royal de l'Afrique Centrale, Tervuren 100–1; National Galleries of Scotland 45b; National Portrait Gallery, London 21; Orleans House Gallery, Twickenham 34l, 34r, 50, 51al, 51b, 109, 112, 113a; Roger-Viollet 16bl, 23b, 31b, 32b, 67, 83, 91b, 94, 94–5c, 95b, 97, 115b, 116–7, 118, 129, 150, 150–1, 153; Royal Geographical Society, London, 13, 33, 35r, 36a, 48a, 48r, 52, 53al, 58–9, 60–1, 63a, 64–5, 73c, 102a, 105a, 115a, 123b, 145, 160, spine, back cover; Scala 18–9; Tapabor-de-Selva 31a, 110–1b, 116; Tapabor-Kharbine 19b, 30b, 54–5b, 96b, 114, 122, 126, 149, 162; United Society for the Propagation of the Gospel, London 16br, 24–5, 26–7, 92, 110a. Map on p. 166: Patrick Mérienne

Acknowledgments

The author and publishers wish to thank the following: in England, Mrs. Erica Graham OBE, the keepers of the Orleans House Gallery, Twickenham, the United Society for the Propagation of the Gospel, London, and Eileen Tweedy; in Paris, Emmanuel Picault and Maria Bianchini at *L'Autre Journal*, Laurent Manoeuvre and Philippe Avenier of the Joconde information service of the Musées de France

Anne Hugon, a young historian, has worked
for several years on the history of African exploration and
has translated Mary Kingsley's account of her travels into
French. She teaches at the University of Lyon II and is
writing a thesis on missionaries in Africa.

Translated from the French by Alexandra Cambell

Project Manager: Sharon AvRutick
Typographic Designer: Elissa Ichiyasu
Cover Designer: Robert McKee
Editorial Assistant: Jennifer Stockman
Design Assistant: Penelope Hardy

Library of Congress Catalog Card Number: 92–82806

ISBN 0–8109–2810–8

Published in 1993 by Harry N. Abrams, Incorporated, New York
A Times Mirror Company

Printed and bound in Italy by Editoriale Libraria, Trieste